A Chinese
KITCHEN

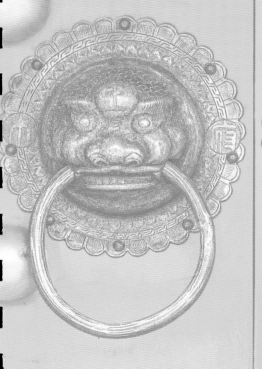

Star★Advertiser
HAWAI'I Cooks
A Chinese KITCHEN

Traditional Recipes with an Island Twist

LYNETTE LO TOM

Photography by
Kaz Tanabe

Mutual
Publishing

This book is warmly dedicated to my mother,
Lorna Hung Kee Lee Lo, who is a great cook.
When I was 11, she asked me to make dinner for the family.
She taught me to love the art of cooking and to share love through food.

Library of Congress Control Number: 2015942561

ISBN: 978-1939487-52-0

Food photography by Kaz Tanabe
Art direction by Jane Gillespie
Interior design by Courtney Tomasu

First Printing, September 2015

Mutual Publishing, LLC
1215 Center Street, Suite 210
Honolulu, Hawai'i 96816
Ph: 808-732-1709 / Fax: 808-734-4094
email: info@mutualpublishing.com
www.mutualpublishing.com

Printed in South Korea

Photo/art credits:

Lynette Lo Tom collection: pg. xii, xiii (bottom), xiv, xvi (left), xvii (top), 6 (bottom), 27, 125, 139, 152
© Sohrab Dorabji: pg. x, xxiii (top), xxiv, 77, 166, 190
© Doug Young: pg. xiii (top), xxvi, 3, 12, 63, 74, 75, 109, 184
© Marc Schechter: pg. xviii, xix, xxi, 7
© Bradley Wong: pg. xvi (right), xx, xxii, xxiii (bottom)
© Rebecca Teo: pg. 8, 16
© *Honolulu Star-Advertiser*: pg. 49 (by Bruce Asato), 68 (by Dennis Oda), 173 (by Cindy Ellen Russell)
© Foodland: pg. 51, 148
© Lei-Sanne Doo: pg. 20, 61
© Komagome family: pg. 89
© Hung Won Restaurant: pg. 137
© Tsung Tsin Association: pg. 154
© Megan Tomino: pg. 162-164
© Sig Zane: pg. 170 (lychee)

Photos from Dreamstime.com:
pg. i © Blagodeyatel, pg. v © Winai Tepsuttinun, pg. vi © Rangizzz, pg. xii © Kschua, pg. xviii (photo background) © Liligraphie, pg. 1 © Dariusz Kopestynski, pg. 5 © Zygotehasnobrain, pg. 7 © Tachjang, pg. 10 © Woravit Vijitpanya, pg. 11 © Somyot Pattana, pg. 30 © Pichest Boonpanchua, pg. 33 © Felinda, pg. 40 © Kewuwu, pg. 41 © Feng Hui, pg. 43 © Nevinates, pg. 59 © Somchaip, pg. 81 © Dejia Gao, pg. 89 (photo frame) © Dejia Gao, pg. 91 © Louella38, pg. 93 © Evelyn Thomas, pg. 98 © Donkeyru, pg. 100 © Ruben Paz, pg. 114 © Nuttapol Noprujikul, pg. 115 © Dmitry Sytnik, pg. 116 © Buch, pg. 124 © Jedimaster, pg. 126 © Nipaporn Panyacharoen, pg. 127 © Keithwilson, pg. 128 © Ruikang Xu, pg. 128 © Anton Starikov, pg. 129 © Coprid, pg. 141 © © Ruikang Xu, pg. 149 © Tangducminh, pg. 151 © Le-thuy Do, pg. 159 © Nuttapong, pg. 160 © Jianghongyan, pg. 166 (tangerines) © Draftmode, pg. 167 © Smeshinka, pg. 170 (almonds) © Sally Scott, pg. 171 © Ppy2010ha

Star ★ Advertiser

HONOLULU

Chinese Kitchen is the fourth in a series from Mutual Publishing and the *Honolulu Star-Advertiser* exploring Hawai'i's many ethnic cuisines.

The aim of this series is to showcase writers who grew up in Hawai'i and learned the dishes of their heritage, local-style. Theirs are no-nonsense, home-style recipes meant to be referred to again and again when you are cooking for your own family.

Our latest author, Lynette Lo Tom, is perfect for this series, sharing her lifelong devotion to Chinese cooking in stories, recipes and historic accounts. Her book will make you yearn for a platter of kau yuk.

At the *Honolulu Star-Advertiser* we celebrate the diversity of island cuisine every week on our Food pages. We are proud to build on that tradition with the series "Hawai'i Cooks."

Dennis Francis
President and Publisher,
Honolulu Star-Advertiser and O'ahu Publications

Contents

前菜 / 小食
Appetizers

湯
Soups

雞絲米粉湯	Chicken Long Rice	25
酸辣湯	Hot and Sour Soup	26
瑤柱羹	Dried Scallop Soup	27
冬瓜湯	Winter Melon Soup	28
雲吞	Won Ton Soup	31
雞肉白菜薑湯	Chicken Napa Cabbage Ginger Soup	33
中式火鍋以及配料	Chinese Hot Pot Soup and Dipping Sauces	35
雞酒	Chicken Soup with Ginger and Whiskey	38
西洋菜湯	Watercress and Pork Soup	40

猪肉
Pork

酸甜排骨	Sweet and Sour Pork Spareribs	42
菠蘿古老肉	Sweet and Sour Spareribs with Pineapple and Green Pepper	43
叉燒	*Char Siu* / Chinese Barbecued Pork	44
叉燒五花腩肉	Char Siu Pork Belly	45
叉燒排骨	Char Siu Spareribs	46
燒豬肉	Crispy Skin Roast Pork	48
豆豉排骨	Black Bean Spareribs	50
椒鹽豬排	Pepper Salt Pork Chops	51
魷魚蒸肉餅	Steamed Pork Hash with Dried Squid	53
燒肉	*Kau Yuk with Taro* / Chinese Pot Roast Pork	54
木须肉	*Mu Shu Pork* / Shredded Pork and Vegetables	56
獅子頭	Lion's Head	57
豬腳醋	Sweet and Sour Pig's Feet	58

鱼類
Fish and Seafood

雞鴨類
Poultry

薏米填鴨	Barley Duck	92
陳皮白果鴨	Duck with Gingko Nut	95
	and Dried Orange Peel	95
檸檬雞	Lemon Chicken	97

豆腐和雞蛋
Tofu & Eggs

蒸釀豆腐	Steamed Stuffed Tofu	100
蝦米豆腐	Cold Tofu with Dried Shrimp	101
涼拌腐竹	Tossed Foo Jook Salad	102
麻婆豆腐	*Ma Po Dou Foo* / Spicy Cooked Tofu	104
魚豆腐	Easy Tofu and Gluten	105
炸釀豆腐	Mānoa Valley	
	Stuffed Fried Bean Curd	107
海鮮腐皮卷	Shrimp Fried Dried Bean Curd Roll	108
蒸蛋羹	Steamed Eggs	109
鹹蛋	Salted Eggs	110
皮蛋	Preserved or 1,000-Year-Old Eggs	113
皮蛋韭菜炒蛋	Pei Dan with Chives and Egg	114
茶葉蛋	Chinese Tea Eggs	115

牛肉
Beef

番茄牛肉	Beef Tomato	117
炆牛百葉	Tripe Stew	118
苦瓜牛肉	Beef with Bitter Melon	121
蒙古牛肉	Mongolian Beef	123
炆牛尾	Oxtail Stew	124
牛肉芥蘭	Beef Broccoli or Chinese Broccoli	126
炆牛舌	Stewed Beef Tongue	127

飯麵類
Rice and Noodles

素菜
Vegetables

甜点
Sweets

Acknowledgments

"Sorry, can't give you that recipe. It's a family secret."

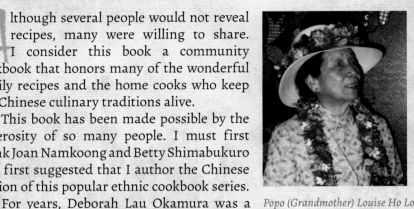

Popo (Grandmother) Louise Ho Lo

Although several people would not reveal recipes, many were willing to share. I consider this book a community cookbook that honors many of the wonderful family recipes and the home cooks who keep our Chinese culinary traditions alive.

This book has been made possible by the generosity of so many people. I must first thank Joan Namkoong and Betty Shimabukuro who first suggested that I author the Chinese version of this popular ethnic cookbook series.

For years, Deborah Lau Okamura was a strong advocate who believed that I could delve into the culinary world. Taren Taguchi gave constant encouragement and valuable input, and Yen Chun provided hours of advice on Chinese language, translations and culture.

In addition to the many contributors (you'll see their names with their recipes), so many friends, old and new, shared their cookbooks and family recipes or offered help in many ways, including:

Henry Adaniya, Kelsi Ikeda Akahoshi, Linda Lau Anusasananan, Cookie Doo Ayabe, Carolyn Yap Ballou, Koreen Barfield, Lisa Baxa, Cheryl Bochentin, Max and Marivic Borromeo, Dave Caldiero, Charlene Lo Chan, Eddie Chan and Winnie Hui, Tina Chang, Claire Chao, Donna Ching, Eldon Ching, Doug Chong and the volunteers at the Hawai'i Chinese History Center, Mel Choy and Gayle Choy Chang, Michele Ching Choy, Clayton Chu, Bina Chun, Glenna Clegg, Herb and Nancy Conley, Denby Fawcett, Sandra Au Fong, Juliet Garcia, Joanne Lo Grimes, Elmer Guzman, Tony Hall, Vienna Hao of Kirin Restaurant, Ann Harakawa, Karin Hatcher, Howard Hu, Debbie Hirai, Sylvia Liang Ho and Gary Chan of Jade Dynasty Restaurant, Caron Ikeda, Dot Iwamoto, Wayne Iwaoka, Elise Jang, Lilia Kapuniai, Christina Kemmer, Ed Kenney, Lloyd and Diana Komagome, Kalowena and Kawena Komeiji, Melanie Kosaka, Nira Luke Low Kurihara, Alison Kwok, Suzanne Watanabe Lai, Patricia Linda Lau, Bonni Sue Lee, Edgy Lee, Fred Lee, Helen

Noh Lee, Laurie Jean Lee, Bill Leung and Casey Kwok of Fook Yuen Restaurant, Kevin Li of Hung Won Restaurant, Adele Low, Sharon Lo Lucien, Warren and Carolyn Luke, Frankie Ma, Maile Meyer, Richie Miao and Xiao Mei Miu, Dore Minatodani, Sandy Moribe, Tsu-i Mullinax, Eleanor Nakama-Mitsunaga, Jean Nakanishi, Gloria Nakea, Lily Ning, Regino Ojano III, Melanie Okazaki, Joleen Oshiro, Lani Parry, Judy Pietsch, Kaui Philpotts, Robert Riggs, Karen Robertshaw, Ray Seto, Bob Sigall, Jay and Carrie Talwar, Allie Tamanaha, Floyd Takeuchi, Sheryl Toda, Joyce Tomonari, June Tong, Barbara Tongg, Anita Li Truong of Welcome Market, Roger and Jenai Wall, Wennie Wang, Stan and Myrna Watanabe, Christie Wilson, Elizabeth Winternitz, Laurie Hong Wong, Shirley and Yuen Wong, Alvin Yee, Ian Yee, Jolly Young, Roger Yu and Carole Goodson, Allena Eimi Zecha, Kana Zheng and Chef De Hui Liang of Mini Garden Restaurant.

I am sorry that all the suggested recipes couldn't be included.

Many helped with art and the look of the book including:

Lynette with Thomas "L.P." Lo, a grand-uncle at his birthday party at Wo Fat.

Mian Cui, Lei-Sanne Doo, Sohrab Dorabji, Dawn MacNaughton, Malcolm Mekaru, Marc Schecter, Floyd Takeuchi, Kaz Tanabe, Megan Tomino, Allen Murabayashi, Rebecca Teo, Bradley Wong, Sidney Yee and Saedene Yee Ota, and Doug Young.

Appreciation goes to wonderful editors Betty Shimabukuro and Muriel Miura and those at Mutual Publishing, including Bennett Hymer, Gay Wong, Jane Gillespie, and Courtney Tomasu.

> *"You could eat Chinese food three meals a day for all of your life and not repeat a dish. There are that many combinations."*
>
> —THE LATE FRANKIE CHUNG OF KAUA'I, A CHINESE FOOD AFICIONADO, AS TOLD TO MELANIE OKAZAKI.

The recipes came alive at the photo shoot with the help of the Leeward Community College Asian Food culinary star students and chef-instructors David Millen and Matt Egami.

In Zhongshan, China, my research was made possible through the generosity of Yen Chun, Victor Sun, and the Zhongshan Foreign and Overseas Chinese Affairs Bureau with Section Chief Gan Huanzhang and the wonderful interpreter and Deputy Section Chief Gavin Yao, and his wife, Vivian Lo. Restaurant managers and chefs were generous with their knowledge of the cuisine, including Zhang Wei Xiong of Shiqi Lo Restaurant, Johnson Soong of Zhongshan Broadcasting, Yuun Xiuy Qiong, general manager of Seaport City Seafood Restaurants, and Fuhua Hotels Food and Beverage Director Huang Ruikan.

My research visits to Taiwan, Hong Kong, and Singapore were spectacular because of: Dennis and Lynette Chen, Deborah Yu Cooney, Charles and Jooeun Kwak, Cassandra Pan, Rebecca Teo, and John and Grace Wang.

I am very appreciative of all those who were giving of their family stories, cooking tips, and introductions to others who enjoy Chinese food. Please forgive me if I didn't include your name.

Lynette with her parents, Lorna and Richard Lo, at Wo Fat Restaurant in 1957.

Lastly, much appreciation goes to my husband, Neal Ken Kanda, who was a taste tester, gave his thumbs up and thumbs down and supported me on this project, daughter Jenny Tom, who constantly gives me encouragement, and of course, my mother, who gives honest feedback when she tells me how to "doctor it up!"

Mahalo!

The Hawai'i Cooks Series

Lynette Lo Tom may well be the most passionate student of any cuisine that we have ever met. She grew up in a family of great cooks and has built on that background throughout her life, studying, experimenting, interviewing, and generally eating up (pardon the pun) all she can learn about Chinese food and cooking. A trip to China is for her not so much a vacation as a chance to learn even more, right at the source.

Lynette was the ideal choice for *A Chinese Kitchen*, the fourth book in the "Hawai'i Cooks" series. A dedicated and accomplished home cook who takes her recipes seriously, Lynette presents a collection of great variety, covering Chinese cooking as it has been adapted and adopted in our islands.

We hope that you will get out the chopsticks and dig in.

Betty Shimabukuro and Muriel Miura
Editors

A Note on Spellings

Although Chinese characters are understood by all throughout the Chinese diaspora, romanization, or the method of translating the characters into English words, varies by system and by region. There are three main systems: Yale, Wade-Giles and Pinyin. The Pinyin system was official adopted by China in 1979. Many of the spellings in this cookbook use the older Yale and Wade-Giles spellings in Cantonese, which are more familiar to Hawai'i Chinese. Also, some pronunciations are in the Hakka dialect.

Lynette's great-grandfather, Wong Tin Look, in a 1912 photo.

His wife, Tom Sai Jun, in 1957. She had bound feet.

A Note on Word Usage

When writing a Chinese cookbook, one is faced with word style, copyediting and spelling complexity. Within the many regions of China, the names of ingredients and dishes vary. Even within one region, such as southern China, there are many dialects. As a result, a dish can be called several names. We have not always provided the Chinese name along with the English name when there were several choices. We tried in the recipe header to indicate the most common usage in Hawaii, which was usually the Cantonese pronunciation.

The glossary is all encompassing to accommodate the many culinary terms used. Besides Chinese, ingredients from Hawaii's other ethnic cuisines and even a few general unusual non-ethnic ones were included. We indicated in parenthesis the Chinese ingredients when they first appear.

Lynette's maternal grandmother, Florence Wong Lee (right) and her sister Esther Chow Ho Chun (left). Florence and Esther loved to cook Chinese food and dance hula together.

It is impossible not to have non-food Chinese words in a recipe book like this. Because of their frequency, we didn't want to bog the text down with definitions, translations, or put the words in italics, thus they are in the glossary.

Thank you for your understanding.

Introduction

What makes a dish Chinese? And what makes it a Hawai'i-Chinese preparation? For two years I've been asking people about Chinese food and this cookbook is a result of the feedback I've received.

I must tell you that I am not an expert in Chinese history or Chinese culinary arts, nor am I a professional chef. But I have been eating Hawai'i-style Chinese cooking for nearly 60 years and am fortunate to come from a family of many good cooks. Food was and still is a very important part of our lives. This cookbook started as a quest for me to document the delicious foods of my paternal grandmother, Louise "Ah Kim" Ho

Chinatown, Honolulu.

Lo; my maternal grandfather, John (Duck) Sau Lee; and my mother, Lorna Lee Lo. It has expanded to include hundreds of contributions from generous people who donated recipes and stories about the foods that they enjoy.

In Hawai'i, mention favorite Chinese foods and four out of five times, Cantonese dishes will be named. Until about 30 years ago, almost all Chinese in the state had roots in Southern China, so it makes sense that foods from the Guangdong (Canton) area have been predominant. Specifically, most Chinese plantation workers were from a small area in Guangdong then called Heong Shan (Fragrant Mountain) and now called Zhongshan, in honor of Dr. Sun Yat-Sen. It's an area just north of Macao.

Cantonese food can be the most expensive in the world or the cheapest, according to award-winning Food and Beverage Director Huang Ruikun of Zhongshan's famous FuHua Hotel restaurants. Many traditional foods use inexpensive ingredients and what we Westerners would consider "throw-away" parts of animals, so the peasant class could feed their families with vegetables, rice, and just a small portion of meat or fish—and if that were not available, tofu.

"You cannot talk food in Mandarin. Cantonese is the language of Chinese food."

—Dr. Daniel Kwok,
retired University of Hawai'i
Professor of Chinese History

On the other side of the spectrum, Chef Huang speaks of the demand for the

"Cantonese food must be: fresh, original, tender, and smooth."

—Zhang Wei Xiong,
owner of Zhongshan's famous
Shiqi Lo (Local Guys) restaurant

freshest and most rare ingredients by those who could afford them (e.g., the Imperial Court), centuries ago and today. These delicacies include the freshest foods from the sea, such as abalone, lobster, sea cucumber (beche de mer), shark's fin, all forms of shellfish, and specific types of fish such as grouper, rock cod, flounder, and certain snappers. Land delicacies include the rare bird's nests, actually the saliva from birds of a certain region, rare mushrooms, and cuts of the favored meat of the South—pork.

There are said to be eight or nine regional types of food in China, but within each region are thousands of styles and sub-regional specialties. The Chinese are pragmatic people. If their village had an abundance of peanuts, peanuts were included in their jook (savory rice gruel), soups, and desserts.

Overall, however, Chinese cuisine favors certain ingredients: tea, ginger, Chinese parsley, pork, rice, five spice, white pepper, star anise, black mushrooms, cloud ear fungus, preserved vegetables of all varieties, fresh and dried tofu, fermented shrimp paste, Chinese dry sausages, and preserved eggs. Adding any of these ingredients brings to mind Chinese flavors.

Certain traditional combinations of foods—with set seasonings and preparations—go back centuries. Amazingly, some dishes have not changed. Pot roast pork belly (kau yuk) with taro is prepared today by frying, braising and steaming with the same fermented red bean sauce that I believe was used during the Ching dynasty. A simple vinegar, salt, and sugar pickle using inexpensive mustard cabbage (tsin choy) stir-fried with slivered pieces of pork is depicted in Zhongshan museums as typical food of the 18th century.

Still, food is constantly evolving. Hawai'i's famous cake noodle is similar to fried noodles in China, but has been adapted to use saimin noodles, themselves a combination of Chinese and Japanese influences. Also, the fried noodle cakes are made thicker in Hawai'i than anywhere in China. With today's access to ingredients from around the

Honolulu's Chinatown Market.

globe, vegetables unavailable to the Chinese centuries ago have been incorporated with old-style sauces, yielding such dishes as Black Bean Asparagus.

While the majority of Hawai'i's Chinese hail from Zhongshan, the influences of other regions have added to the richness of our Chinese food. Some of the most popular dishes today are not Cantonese—Ma Po Tofu, Honey Walnut Shrimp, Pepper Salt Pork Chops or Calamari, Green Onion Fried Bread, and dishes using the classic Sichuan spice, the mouth-numbing peppercorn.

OIS house on Fort Street, Honolulu
at the Time of grandfather's
birthday celebration.
1898

Hawai'i's Chinese food also has achieved a wonderful richness born of an intersection of cultures. Fried rice, for example, can include Portuguese sausage, Filipino pork adobo and a spicy dip made from Japanese wasabi mustard. Artist Sig Zane adds kim chee to his pork hash-stuffed fried tofu.

The reverse is also true. Given the number of marriages between native Hawaiians and Chinese, many traditional Chinese foods are considered local Hawaiian standards, such as Chicken Long Rice, Beef Tomato and Chop Steak.

Lynette's great-great-grandfather's Fort Street house at the time of his birthday celebration in 1898.

Tastes are personal, so each family will have different ingredients and proportions for the same dish. There is no right or wrong.

I hope that you will enjoy these recipes as much as I've enjoyed researching them. And I hope that some of the stories told in this book will bring back memories of food from your Goong Goong (grandfather) or Popo (grandmother).

Share your love through cooking. Xie xie (Mandarin), um gwei (Cantonese dialect), do sia (Hakka dialect), and mahalo,

"Life is short, so let's get cooking!"

Lynette CoTon

The Chinese in Hawai'i

"When you eat fruit, think of the tree that bore it.
When you drink water, think of its source."

—Yu Xin, SIXTH-CENTURY SCHOLAR

This centuries-old saying illustrates a strong root of Chinese philosophy. Our fortunes today are rooted in the past, and based on the sacrifices our ancestors made.

Although Chinese and part-Chinese represent only about 13 percent of Hawai'i's overall population according to the latest census, China's rich culture has contributed much to the identity and lifestyle of the islands, especially to our cuisine.

Like most immigrants, the Chinese came to Hawai'i to escape political and economic conditions in their homeland, drawn by the promise of a better life overseas. Powerful business leaders required cheap labor to power the lucrative sugar

Chinatown, Honolulu.

industry as the native Hawaiian population had been decimated by diseases brought by foreigners.

To the poor and mostly uneducated workers from southern China, a contract to work in the fields for three to five years sounded like a good way to provide for their children.

The Chinese were the first wave of plantation laborers, and their influence on our state's foods and tastes remains strong.

No one knows the date that the first Chinese arrived, but it was likely around 1778, when a trading ship came to Hawai'i with Chinese cooks and sailors aboard. It is suspected that several jumped ship and stayed, as subsequent visitors made note of Asian-looking children in Hawai'i.

In China at the time—the Qing (Ching) Dynasty—conditions were terrible for the poor, especially in the south. There was much corruption, especially among government officials, and many families could not survive.

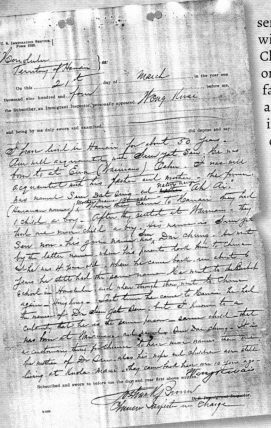

Letter from Wong Kwai vouching for Sun Yat-Sen.

It was common for families to send their sons to other lands to work, with the hope that they would return to China with the money to build houses or businesses that would benefit the family. Many left hoping to provide a better life for their offspring. Some intended to return to the homeland, others knew they couldn't survive in southern China.

Beginning in the late 18th century there were many arrivals from China, some documented, some not. From 1802 through 1814, when sugar mills were started on Kauaʻi and Lānaʻi, the Chinese were sought for their expertise in growing and processing sugar. Southern China's climate is similar to Hawaiʻi's and sugar cane was already being grown there.

Some early Chinese arrivals started independent sugar mills, but only a few succeeded because of a lack of laborers and funding.

In the 1840s and '50s missionaries from New England revived Hawaiʻi's sugar and rice industries and brought over an initial group of Chinese from Fukien province as plantation hands. For whatever reason they didn't work out. Mill owners then gave a few of the earliest Chinese immigrants incentives to recruit their countrymen.

One of those recruiters was my maternal great-great-grandfather, Wong Kwai, who turned to family and friends from his hometown, the village of Punsa (Ban Shan in Mandarin, or "sandy peninsula"); the larger area of See Dai Doo, above Macao; and below Canton, in the area called Heong Shan (Fragrant Mountain).

It's estimated that 75 to 80 percent of Hawaiʻi's plantation workers came from the Heong Shan area, which is why most Chinese food in Hawaiʻi reflects what is called Cantonese food, and more specifically, the preferences of the smaller region of Heong Shan. In 1927, Heong Shan was

Chinese in Hawaiʻi

renamed Zhongshan, in honor of China's first president, Dr. Sun Yat-Sen (one of his names was Zhongshan).

Kohala Tong Wo Society, founded 1886.

Unlike some later groups of immigrants to Hawai'i, most workers from China were men. Those who were married came alone and sent a portion of their earnings home. Because they were here without women, the plantation arrangement usually included cooks. But when they could, many O'ahu workers would catch a buggy ride to Chinatown, where there were several places to eat the Heong Shan-style of food that they craved.

Workers were sent to work on almost every island: Kohala and Ka'ū on Hawai'i island, O'ahu, Kaua'i, Maui and Lāna'i.

According to all accounts, it was brutal physical work in the brutal sun with long hours. An overseer who wasn't Chinese would whip the laborers if they weren't going fast enough. Management's strategy was to bring in mixed ethnic groups, keep them separated as much as possible, and play them against each other to keep from uniting against the Caucasian owners and managers.

According to one estimate, about half the laborers returned to China after their contracts ended. Those who stayed in Hawai'i continued as vegetable and rice farmers, or as merchants. Many moved to Honolulu's Chinatown to set up restaurants, laundries, and shops.

Near Chinatown, you'll see the buildings established by the benevolent societies that the laborers founded with others from their same villages. At first these

Lynette's maternal great-grandfather and family in Honolulu in 1898.

societies were open to men only, but gradually women and families were included. There now are seven village groups, or "doos," as some have merged since the 19th century, with names like

See Dai Doo, Gook Doo, Loong Doo and Leong Doo.

Today's young Chinese in Hawai'i could be sixth- or seventh-generation Americans, counting in the Chinese way, which counts the first generation as those people who left China.

The Chinese further contributed to Hawai'i's food culture through the plants they introduced to the island. Y. Baron Goto, former director of the Hawai'i Agricultural Extension Service at the University of Hawai'i, lists these plants as among the many that are Chinese in origin:

- **Fruits:** Lychee, longan, lime, pomelo, certain varieties of mango, and Chinese varieties of peach, kumquat, persimmon, and sand pear.

- **Vegetables:** Arrowroot, bamboo, bean sprouts, bitter melon, bok choy, dish cloth gourd (Chinese okra or see gwa), green onions, ling gok (the dark brown pod that resembles steer horns), lotus root, mustard cabbage, peas, soy beans, swamp cabbage, turnip, water chestnuts, winter melon, and Chinese varieties of cabbage, chives, parsley, spinach, taro, and yam.

- **Flowers:** Chrysanthemums, eagle claw, gardenia, hydrangea, honeysuckle, jasmine (called pikake in Hawai'i), lotus, narcissus, pak lan, Chinese violet (called pakalana in Hawai'i), and ylang ylang.

Narcissus plant

Over the past 30 years, foods from other regions of China have joined the primarily Cantonese-style, simple village food that was the root of local-style Chinese cuisine. Foods from Sichuan, Shanghai, and northern China have become more commonplace.

Through the 1970s it was rare to find Onion Bread (Chung Yao Beng), Honey Walnut Shrimp, or Spicy Tofu (Ma Po Dou Foo) on a restaurant menu. Now those dishes are offered routinely.

The Hawai'i experience regarding Chinese food is common. Overseas Chinese communities around the world are estimated at more than 36 million, with many of those communities sharing the ancestral homeland of Guangdong (province of Canton). So what the world knows most is Cantonese food.

Chinese Cooking Methods

there are about a dozen standard Chinese cooking methods and many more that combine two or more of the techniques below.

- **Stir-frying** (chao) is thought of as the classic Chinese way to cook. Ingredients are cut into uniform pieces and constantly stirred over high heat.

- **Steaming** (ching) is used more by the Chinese than many other cultures. Food is put in a bowl or platter above boiling water, resulting in very tender food with a delicate texture. Several tiers may be used, so many dishes can be cooked simultaneously.

- **Poaching** (jum) is a gentle method of cooking, using water or seasoned stock over low heat. It is especially good with fragile foods such as fish.

- **Boiling** (chu), generally a slow boil, is usually used for soups. The ingredients and water are brought to a boil, then the temperature is lowered, and cooking continues for hours, so the essence of the key ingredient is transferred to the liquid. Parboiling is also used to prepare vegetables before stir-frying them.

- **Cold-mixing** (lung ban): Ingredients are parboiled, then mixed together.

- **Smoking** (fen), or smoking with tea (cheong cha), is a method used to provide smoky flavor to foods.

- **Barbecuing** (shu) is usually done outdoors, but also in an oven.

- **Roasting** (kau) can be done in an oven, but in olden days, was done outside over a fire.

- **Pan- or shallow-frying** (chien) uses less oil than deep-frying and at a lower temperature. Foods are fried on one side and then turned over to brown on the other.

- **Deep-frying** (tsa, zhai) uses a quantity of oil heated to 350 to 375°F. Peanut oil, which can reach a high temperature without smoking, is the traditional choice. (Today, peanut allergies are more common, so know your guests.) Thicker pieces of meat must be steamed, then dried, before deep-frying or they risk being raw inside and burnt outside.

- **Red-cooking or stewing** (hung shu) means braising with a strong-colored soy sauce and other spices until the food darkens. Meats or tofu are cooked with this method, said to be unique to the Chinese.

- **Clay pot or casserole cooking** (bo zai) is common in winter. A sandy clay pot or ceramic casserole is filled with liquid and slowly heated over a charcoal fire or on the stove. Meats or vegetables are added with spices to make delicious stews, soups or braised foods.

Mānoa Chop Suey

前菜 / 小食
Appetizers

It is at Chinese formal banquets that appetizers are showcased. As in other cuisines, the first course gives a preview of the meal to come. Traditionally the appetizer platter is served at room temperature and is a combination of types of food that whet your appetite for more. These dishes usually will not reappear during the dinner. So if Cantonese duck or Peking duck is served as part of the banquet, it will not be on the appetizer platter.

Selections could include marinated and braised lamb or beef shank slices, pickled vegetables or seasoned peanuts, choice pieces of roast pork or barbecue meat (char siu), duck, squab, chicken or prepared delicacies such as duck's tongues or web, chicken feet or leaf tripe with slices of raw chili pepper.

At home, families sit down to multiple courses served all at once and appetizers are seldom offered.

During local parties, many Chinese dishes are appetizers, including Hawai'i's favorites—fried won ton or gau gee, char siu pork or spareribs and the beloved small bundle of pork hash.

Other "small bites" take the form of snacks, and the Chinese love them, from simple boiled peanuts with a touch of star anise flavor to the complex preserved forms of salty-sweet dried fruits that Hawai'i has come to love.

可樂豉油雞翼
Cola Soy Sauce Chicken Wings

From Yang Jia

Makes 8 servings as an appetizer

Yang Jia, a Mandarin teacher with the Confucius Institute at the University of Hawai'i's Outreach College, says this is one of the most popular dishes among young people in China today. Only the middle part of the wings are used in China (save the drumsticks for another dish and the tips for soup stock). Here in Hawai'i we use all parts.

1½ pounds midsection of the chicken wings, cut at joints
2 tablespoons vegetable oil
1 can of cola (12 ounces, not diet)
4 teaspoons soy sauce
1 tablespoon Shaoxing wine or dry sherry
Garnish: chopped green onions (optional)

Wash and clean the chicken. Drain the chicken wings on paper towels for at least 20 minutes to dry them. In a large skillet, heat oil and fry chicken in batches until both sides are browned. Combine all chicken pieces in skillet with cola, soy sauce and wine and bring to a boil, then reduce heat. Simmer on low heat until liquid is gone as chicken should be tender by then. Garnish with green onions and serve.

Feeds How Many?

Serving sizes given with the recipes in this book are in the Western style dining, where you have one main dish served with a starch. In the Chinese home, it is traditional to serve one dish per person, not counting rice or a soup. So for a family of five, you would serve five different dishes, plus rice and soup.

Maunakea Street, Chinatown.

涼拌海蜇
Jellyfish Salad
Makes 8 servings as an appetizer

½ pound salted jellyfish, soaked in water and refrigerated overnight

Water to soak and rinse jellyfish

½ cup cucumber, seeded and slivered

½ cup turnip, slivered

1¼ teaspoons salt, divided

1 tablespoon soy sauce

1 teaspoon sugar

¼ teaspoon ground white pepper

1 tablespoon white vinegar

1 teaspoon sesame oil

Drain soaked jellyfish and shred into long pieces. Place in cold water and cover for 1 hour, changing water once. Remove and drain.

Toss cucumber and turnip slivers with ¼ teaspoon salt.

In another bowl, mix together the remaining salt, soy sauce, sugar, pepper, vinegar and sesame oil. Mix in jellyfish. Let marinate a few hours.

On a serving platter, place the drained cucumber and turnip slivers on a serving plate. Place jellyfish on top of cucumbers and turnip with the marinade. Serve immediately or chill for a few hours.

Chinese Banquets

At formal banquets, eight or ten diners are seated at a round table, so each person is equal distance across the table.

Huang Ruikun, food and beverage director of Zhonghan's FuHua Hotel restaurants explained to me the order of the dishes in the meal:

The first course is a cold (or room temperature) platter of appetizers, such as Chinese roast pig (siu ji yuk), jellyfish, braised beef tendon or shin meat, tea eggs, barbecued pork (char siu), pickled vegetables, and possibly chicken gizzards.

The second course is soup. It could be a double-boiled chicken, birds-nest, winter melon, or dried scallop soup.

The third course should showcase the most expensive item of the night, to impress the guests. Is it a rare fish steamed whole with ginger, green onions, and Chinese parsley? The coveted abalone, sea cucumber, "hairy crab" or in China—shark's fin?

The fourth course is the second most expensive item, followed by a vegetable, then the third most expensive item. Seventh is a form of rice or noodle, then a dessert.

Each dish should feature a different cooking style—pan-frying, deep-frying, smoking, braising, steaming, stir-frying, boiling, pickling, salting, or simmering.

涼拌牛百葉
Tripe "Poke"

From Lorna Lo
Makes 6 servings as an appetizer

*E*very time my mother serves this at parties, people enjoy it because it is rarely served. The key to the dish is its crunchy texture, as the tripe itself is quite bland.

> 1 pound leaf (not honeycomb) tripe, also called book tripe
> 1 tablespoon baking soda*
> Water to cover tripe
> 2-inch piece ginger, finely slivered
> 3 stalks green onion, slivered
> ¼ cup chopped Chinese parsley
> 1 jalapeño chili pepper, finely slivered (optional)

Dipping sauce:
> 1 tablespoon dry Chinese hot mustard
> 1 tablespoon water
> ½ teaspoon oil
> 2 tablespoons soy sauce

Cut leaf part of tripe into bite-sized pieces. Cut thicker part of tripe into strips. Put tripe in a bowl and massage ("lomi lomi") with the baking soda or lye water. Let sit for 2 hours. Place tripe in a colander, located in the sink, and gently run cold water over for 30 minutes.

Put tripe in pot with enough water to cover. Bring to a boil and cook for 5 minutes. Take out thinner leaf tripe and drain. The thicker strips may need to boil for 2 to 3 more minutes. Drain. Put on serving platter and top with ginger, green onions, Chinese parsley, and chili. Refrigerate until served.

Serve with a dipping sauce of Chinese hot mustard, water, oil and soy sauce.

* You can substitute 1 tablespoon lye water if you have it.

釀冬菇
Stuffed Black Mushrooms

From John Sau Lee
Makes 30

†*he combination of flavors makes this a popular and easy-to-eat appetizer.*

30 large dried black mushrooms
½ pound ground pork
1 pound raw Chinese fish cake
3 stalks green onion,
   minced
½ teaspoon ground white
   pepper
1 tablespoon oyster sauce
2 teaspoons cornstarch diluted
   with 4 tablespoons water
Garnish: Chinese parsley

Soak mushrooms for at least 20 minutes in hot water. Clean off any dirt. Boil in water until soft, about 20 minutes. Cut off stems and keep mushroom caps whole; set aside. Brown the pork in a skillet over low heat; drain any oil. Mix together pork, fish cake, onions and pepper; fill the mushroom caps. Place stuffed mushrooms, meat side up in single layer on heat-proof dish. Steam above boiling water 20 to 30 minutes or until fish cake is cooked. In a saucepan, mix oyster sauce with cornstarch mixture and heat until thickened to make a light gravy. Garnish with Chinese parsley and serve.

Florence and John Sau Lee (Japo and Goong Goong)

煮花生
Boiled Peanuts

From Lorna Lo
Makes 3 pounds

My college roommate, *Terry Doan, offered a fresh perspective on a favorite Hawai'i snack while on a visit from the mainland. "Someone spilled beer over the peanuts and they are all wet," she said. Hawai'i-style peanuts are wet, not dry. Peanuts are prevalent throughout southern China and this recipe includes the popular star anise flavor. Follow the timing and you'll enjoy peanuts with a slight crunch.*

3 pounds raw peanuts in shells
6 quarts water
¾ cup Hawaiian salt
4 whole star anise

Wash and rub raw peanut shells until clean. Rinse and drain. In a large pot, soak peanuts in water, salt and star anise mixture overnight. Weigh down peanuts with a large plate. Twenty-four hours later, heat the pot with the peanuts and the water mixture until it comes to a boil. Cook for 25 to 30 minutes at a high heat. Test one for the texture you like. Drain, cool and refrigerate. Serve. You can prepare this 2 to 3 days in advance and keep refrigerated.

The intersection of N. King St. and Kekaulike St. in Honolulu's Chinatown.

臘腸雲吞 / 餃子
Lup Cheong Gau Gee
From KITV Anchor Pamela Young
Makes about 32 to 36

P amela said she invented this to make a meal out of the ingredients she
had at home!

**4 lup cheong (Chinese
  sweet sausage), diced**
**2 cups mung bean
  sprouts**
**1 pound raw Chinese
  fish cake**
**1 cup chopped green
  onions**
**2 packages (10 ounces
  each) round won ton
  pi (about 20 in each
  package)**
Vegetable oil for frying
Garnish: shiso leaves (beefsteak plant or perilla), optional

Dipping sauce:
Wasabi or hot mustard
Soy sauce

In a skillet, sauté lup cheong until lightly browned on low to medium
heat. Drain on paper towel. Blanch sprouts in boiling water, squeeze out
excess liquid, and chop. In a bowl mix fish cake, lup cheong, bean sprouts,
and onions. Spoon about 2 teaspoons on won ton pi, seal with water,
crimp edges. Deep-fry until crispy and drain on paper towels. Place 2 won
ton pi on a shiso leaf on a plate. Serve with wasabi or hot mustard mixed
with soy sauce on the side.

Tip: If you go to a noodle making shop, you can specify the round, thin
pasta skins (pi), but at most markets, they will sell the thicker, round pi for
Korean mun doo with 16 to a package or the square won ton pi with about
18 to a package.

傳統芒果乾
Old-fashioned Pickled Mango

Makes about 5 quarts

ocal-style. Based on a recipe by the late State Senator Donald Ching.

- **1 cup white vinegar**
- **2 cups sugar**
- **4 tablespoons of Hawaiian salt**
- **5 li hing mui per quart (red ones if you like that old-fashioned red look)**
- **5 to 8 Hawaiian chili peppers, whole or cut**
- **10 to 14 green mangoes**

Simmer pickling liquid of vinegar, sugar, salt, li hing mui and chili peppers. Cool. Peel and slice mangoes and put into a non-reactive container such as a glass jar with a cover; include the seeds too. Leave unrefrigerated for at least 24 hours before serving. This keeps for a long time in the refrigerator. Enjoy.

Popular Chinese saying in Mandarin:
"Chui xian san chi."

Literally:
"Drooling with as much as three feet of saliva."

Meaning:
**Describes the look of someone consumed
with desire, for example, for food.**

楊桃干
Dried Five-Spice Star Fruit Mui

Makes about 20 ounces dried

*C*rack seed—also called cracked seed or preserved fruits—became a local favorite after the Chinese introduced their method of preserving excess fruit. Here is one addicting form of crack seed, a Hilo favorite. The chewy texture and mild five-spice powder flavor will have you eating a bag at a time. Star fruit is also known as carambola.

About 24 medium-sized firm star fruits
5 tablespoons rock salt
2 pounds light brown sugar
¼ cup water
2 teaspoons Chinese five-spice powder
3 tablespoons red food coloring
   (optional)

Wash and slice fruits into ¼-inch slices from end to end so they are shaped like stars. Sprinkle with salt and let stand overnight. Drain. Combine sugar, water, five-spice powder and food coloring (if you are using) and bring to a boil, stirring constantly. Add drained fruit and cook over medium heat for about 20 minutes, stirring occasionally. Cool. Drain excess syrup. Dry the fruits.

Drying methods:

- **Oven method:** Place fruit on flat cookie sheet lined with layers of paper towels. Bake at 170 to 200°F until dry.

- **Sun dry:** For one day

- **Use a dehydrator:** Follow manufacturer's directions.

Seal with a food sealer or zip-top plastic bags and enjoy.

西梅杏乾·
Prune Apricot Mui

Makes 2 quarts

*O*ur family is related to the Chong family of Wing Coffee. Often Mrs. Chong would give me wonderful crack seed from their store on Pauahi Street near Smith Street. I remember long rows of glass jars filled with preserved fruits brought from China. Some had funny names, like football and horse doo doo. The most popular were li hing mui, cherry seed, rock salt plum, wet lemon peel, and my favorite, mango seed. Back in the day the preserves were portioned into paper bags, and after eating, you would turn the bag inside out and lick up every drop of the sweet syrup.

1 pound dark brown sugar
3 tablespoons whiskey
2 tablespoons Hawaiian salt
1 tablespoon Chinese five-spice powder
1 tablespoon ground cloves
1 cup water
3½ pounds dried pitted prunes, cut in half
20 ounces dried apricots, cut in half
½ cup dried lemon peel, cut into pieces and remove seeds
1 cup seedless li hing mui
1½ cups fresh lemon juice

In a large pot, heat the sugar, whiskey, salt, five spice, cloves and water until dissolved. Turn off heat. Add prunes, apricots, lemon peel, li hing mui and lemon juice. Let stand a week at room temperature before eating. This does not need refrigeration.

Wing Coffee Company in Chinatown.

木須肉薄餅
Mandarin Pancakes

Makes 24 pancakes

Y ou may make these ahead of time, or freeze a batch. Reheat by steaming. Use to wrap Mu Shu Pork (see recipe on page 56) or roast duck slices.

1¾ cups all-purpose flour
¾ cup boiling water
Flour for dusting
2 tablespoons vegetable oil

Mix water with flour in a bowl. Turn out onto a floured board. Knead for 3 minutes and cover with a damp cloth. Let rest for 30 minutes. Knead again. Roll out into two cylinders, each 12-inch long and 1-inch in diameter. Cut each cylinder into 24 1-inch pieces. Flatten each piece into a flat pancake about 2 inches in diameter. Brush one side lightly with oil. Place two pancakes together with the oil sides touching. Roll out into 5- to 6-inch pancakes with a rolling pin.

Grill each double pancake in a dry ungreased skillet over low heat. When small bubbles form, flip over and fry an additional minute or two.

Separate the pancakes immediately. Use for Mu Shu Pork or for serving with duck. Separate with waxed or parchment paper before sealing and freezing.

Green Onion Fried Bread

From Linda Chang Wyrgatsch
Makes 6 round bread "pancakes"

I find that adding Sichuan peppercorns adds a tasty spice to this great favorite recipe of many. Linda offers this note: *"Some people prefer to use only a small amount of oil in the pan and cook over low to medium heat. I find that the bread (called Chung Yau Beng) cooks faster and is crispier when fried over higher heat, using more oil. I also prefer my pancakes quite thin, less than ¼ of an inch."*

1¾ cups near-boiling hot water
4 cups flour
10 stalks green onion, chopped, about 2 cups
¼ cup vegetable oil (1 tablespoon can be sesame oil)
2 teaspoons salt
1 teaspoon Sichuan peppercorns, toasted and ground (optional)
2 tablespoons sesame oil
¼ to ⅓ cup vegetable oil

Mix the hot water into the flour. Knead on a well-floured board lightly until a smooth soft dough ball forms. Let the dough rest a minimum of 30 minutes, up to several hours. Do not skip this step. Mix the chopped green onions, oil, salt (and Sichuan peppercorns if you are using it) in a small bowl. Divide the dough into 6 pieces. On a floured surface, roll out one piece into a flat, thin round of approximately 12 inches in diameter. Spread ⅙ of the green onion mixture on the round piece of dough. Using your fingers, roll the dough into a tube shape (like you are rolling up a carpet), coil the tube into a stacked bun shape. Put this aside and repeat the process with the other pieces of dough. Flatten each bun with a rolling pin so each pancake is 10 to 12 inches. (Linda's trick is to put each coiled bun into a large plastic bag and then use a rolling pin to flatten them.) Now you have 6 onion breads ready to cook. Brush them with sesame oil.

Heat oil in a skillet over high heat. Put the onion cake in when the oil is very hot, then reduce the heat to medium. Turn over when crispy brown on one side, in about 3 minutes. Be careful as this burns easily. Cut into 6 to 8 wedges and serve immediately.

湯
Soups

In many Chinese homes, every dinner menu would include a soup. Grandparents would encourage their family members to drink soup because it was good for your cold, for your eyes, for your kidneys, to clear up your complexion or to improve your memory. The list continues.

The culture makes no distinction between soups for medicinal purposes and soups made for nourishment or plain enjoyment. Some soups taste like herbal medicines as they probably are.

Each ingredient is either a symbol of something good or has an ingredient that is said to cure some ailment.

Goji berries are red, a sign of good luck, and they are said to help your blood quality. The black and white fungus (mook ngee) is believed to improve cholesterol. Carrots help your eyes, but the best carrots for soup are the largest ones, which are sweeter than smaller ones. Ginger is good for you always and especially if you are suffering from a cold. Chicken feet will help your arthritis and improve your complexion. Soups with vegetables like watercress or spinach will help your stamina.

In general, a base from clear stocks is most common, made from a wide range of sources including chicken, pork bones, beef bones or shin meat, fish and dried seafood like shrimp, scallops, octopus and squid. The simplest soup can be clear broth with just one other ingredient: watercress, spinach, won bok, squash, fuzzy squash or winter melon. Add a third ingredient and it is an everyday soup: balls of fish cake, dried tofu (foo jook), fresh tofu, tender chicken gizzards or pieces of lotus root. Add more ingredients and it's a fancy soup.

Some soups are a bit thicker, like Hot and Sour Soup or Corn and Chicken Soup. Of course, the rice gruel (jook) is very thick and hearty.

Soups must always be served scalding hot, at least in the Cantonese culture. A sign of a poorly executed restaurant kitchen is a bowl of lukewarm Chinese soup. This is one reason why soup spoons are usually ceramic and more recently plastic, but never made of metal.

鳳爪湯
Chicken Feet Soup

Makes 8 servings

This soup is definitely for the adventurous, although those of us who enjoy the texture of chicken tendons don't understand the squeamishness of others. This is a simple soup with not a strong flavor, but great hot with steamed rice.

1 pound chicken feet (about 16 feet), washed
Water to cover*
2 pieces dried turnip (chung choy)
3 dried black mushrooms
1-inch piece ginger, peeled and sliced
¼ cup peeled and sliced turnip
¼ cup peeled and sliced carrots
1 cup Napa cabbage (won bok) cut in 1-inch pieces
1 teaspoon light soy sauce
¼ teaspoon ground white pepper
Garnishes: chopped green onions and Chinese parsley

Hardy Peasant Stock

The majority of Chinese who came to Hawai'i to work on the plantation were neither nobility nor rich. If they had been wealthy, they would have stayed in China. Our ancestors left their villages so they could make better lives. Some of the phrases commonly used in Hawai'i give away our peasant roots. For example, many of us ask for chicken feet literally as "gai geork," but the higher classes in China and in China-towns throughout the U.S. use the term "fung jow," meaning phoenix claws.

Cut off chicken nails. Put into a pot and cover with water; bring to a boil. Rinse chung choy and add to pot with ginger. Soak dried mushrooms in hot water for at least 30 minutes. Cut off stems and discard, slice mushroom caps thinly. Add to pot.

Cook on medium heat until chicken is tender, about 1 hour 20 minutes. At one hour, add turnips, carrots, won bok, soy sauce and pepper. Skim oil. When chicken feet are tender, skim oil. Serve soup hot with green onions and Chinese parsley as a garnish and have soy sauce on the table for guests to eat with the chicken feet after they have finished the soup.

* Add homemade, canned or boxed chicken broth for a deeper taste.

絲瓜魚丸湯
Silk Squash with Fish Cake Soup
Makes 8 servings

*S*ilk squash also goes by the names loofah, Chinese okra, and see gwa. As substitutes use won bok, watercress, winter melon, mustard cabbage, or spinach. It is delicious and its texture distinct.

2 cups pork spareribs cut into 1-inch pieces (substitute any cut of pork)
4 cups chicken broth
4 cups water
1-inch piece ginger, peeled and sliced
1 piece salted dried turnip (chung choy), rinsed
1 long Chinese silk squash, peeled, not seeded and sliced diagonally,
    about 2 cups
½ teaspoon salt
1 cup Chinese raw fish cake
Garnishes: chopped green onions and Chinese parsley

Combine spareribs, chicken broth, water, ginger and chung choy in a large pot and bring to a boil on high. Reduce heat to medium; cook 1 hour. Add squash and salt; cook 3 minutes. Using a wet teaspoon, drop teaspoons of fish cake into soup. Cook 3 more minutes. Garnish and serve immediately. Do not overcook as squash will fall apart.

牛尾湯
Oxtail Soup for a Crowd

Makes 15 to 20 bowls of soup

My brother Barry's wife, Bunnie Smith Lo, loves vegetables, so when I make oxtail soup for her, I add more vegetables than normal. When I made the soup that way for my mother, she said, "You are missing the point. The best thing about oxtail soup is the broth." As usual, she is right. When this soup is served at parties, the meat is often left over as everyone has seconds of the broth with lots of grated ginger.

8 whole dried black mushrooms
8 dried red dates (hung jo)
1 cup soaked fungus, about 2 dried pieces
15 pounds oxtails, rinsed and fat trimmed off
¾ cup soy sauce
½ cup peeled and sliced fresh ginger root
½ cup dry sherry, whiskey or bourbon
3 tablespoons vegetable oil
Water to cover the oxtails in the pot
12 star anise
1 large piece of dried tangerine peel (gwo pei)
2 pieces (about ¼ cup) chung choy
1 cup raw peanuts, blanched, shelled
6 cups winter melon peeled and cut into ½-inch cubes
2 cups lotus root peeled, sliced ¼-inch thick, and quartered
½ teaspoon white pepper
2 cups turnip, peeled and cut into ¼-inch slices in half or quarters (depends on the width of the turnip)
5 large carrots, peeled and cut into ¼-inch rounds, cut larger pieces in half

Garnishes:
5 inches ginger, peeled and grated to serve with the soup
Green onions, minced
Chinese parsley, minced
1 pound mustard cabbage, cleaned and cut into ½-inch pieces and blanched

In separate bowls, soak the dried ingredients (mushrooms, red dates, fungus) in cold or hot water. Cut as much fat off the oxtails as you can. Soak the meat in the soy sauce, ginger, sherry mixture for at least 15 minutes.

In the largest stock pot you have, heat the oil on high heat. Drain the meat (keep the liquid) and brown the oxtail in small batches. Remove and save meat.

When all the oxtail is browned, put all the meat back into the stockpot, add in the soy sauce mixture and fill the pot with water so the meat is covered by at least a half inch. Add star anise, tangerine peel, chung choy and peanuts.

Cook for 1 hour on medium high heat uncovered. Every 15 minutes skim the oil off the top of the broth and add hot water to keep the meat covered.

Add winter melon, lotus root and white pepper.

Cook 1 hour more. Test meat for doneness. At this point, you may need to remove and set in a bowl the smaller pieces of meat so they are not overdone.

Add turnip and carrots.

Cook for 30 to 60 minutes more, as you test the larger pieces of meat.

You want the meat tender, but not so cooked that it falls off the bone. Add smaller meat pieces back into the pot.

Tip: It's best if you can make this the day before you serve it. Cool and refrigerate. Next day, skim the fat off the top. Reheat. Serve with condiments of grated ginger, green onions, Chinese parsley, and mustard cabbage.

蓮藕湯
Lotus Root Soup

From Lorna Lo
Makes 16 servings as a starter soup or 8 as a main course with rice

Whe we were young we called this *Wagon Wheel Soup*, as the slices of lotus root resemble the spoked wheels of a covered wagon. It was one of our favorite soups as the pork broth merges with the umami-rich taste of the dried squid. Cooked until tender, the lotus root absorbs the broth's flavors and has a great texture.

My father, Richard Cheong Lo, enjoyed the pork bones almost more than the soup itself. I picture him on a Sunday afternoon, pouring soy sauce over a huge bowl of pork bones that my mother pulled from the soup for him. He would savor the morsels of meat left on the soup bones.

2 long segments fresh lotus root (about 4 cups) peeled and cut into
½-inch rounds, then halved, or quartered
½ chung choy, rinsed
½ dried squid (yau ngee) or dried octopus (muk ngee)*
2-inch piece fresh ginger, peeled and smashed
1 piece (1 x 1 inch) dried tangerine peel (gwo pei)
**1 pound pork bones, pork spareribs or pork
shoulder, cut into 1-inch pieces**
3 large dried red dates (4 to 5 smaller ones)
2 tablespoons goji berries, rinsed (optional)**
Water, as needed
¼ pound raw Chinese fish cake
Salt or soy sauce to taste
**Garnishes: chopped green onions and Chinese
parsley**

In a large stock pot, add 3 quarts water and the first 8 ingredients. After this comes to a boil, turn down to medium heat, cover and cook for about 2 hours or until pork and lotus root are tender. Add water to cover ingredients if needed. Skim off any oil, remove dried squid, ginger and chung choy.

(continued on the next page)

Add fish cake in teaspoon-sized balls into soup and cook for a few minutes. Add salt or soy sauce to taste. Add green onions and parsley for garnish. Serve hot.

Note: Like most stews and soups, it's best to make this the day before you want to serve it. The oil will float to the top and will be easy to remove after chilling overnight in the refrigerator.

* Can substitute 5 dried scallops
** Our family's recipe did not include goji berries, but now I see the sweet berries included in restaurant versions because of their health value.

We Miss Tony

The late Anthony Chang was not just an outstanding state senator, but was passionate about Chinese food. For years, he led walking tours of Honolulu's Chinatown and could speak for hours about the diversity and wonder of the restaurant offerings. He said he would never tire of it because the cuisine was so rich and varied, thanks to the country's different climates, geography and cultures. Before his death in 2012, he was working on a story for his book on Chinese food about backyard caterers who would create multi-course banquets after setting up their woks outdoors. His knowledge inspired many of us in Hawai'i to appreciate Chinese food.

Chicken Long Rice

雞絲米粉湯

Makes 6 servings

Chicken Long Rice is so popular that people think it is a local Hawai'i invention, not a Chinese dish. The soup and texture of good long rice noodles make it a comfort food.

- **1 whole chicken (2½ to 3 pounds), including neck and innards**
- **Water to cover**
- **2-inch piece ginger, peeled and sliced**
- **1 piece chung choy**
- **4 black mushrooms, soaked**
- **2 cups winter melon peeled and cubed into ½-inch cubes**
- **1 teaspoon white or black ground pepper**
- **2 packages (7.75 ounces each) Chinese long rice noodles, soaked in hot water for 30 minutes***
- **½ cup green onions, chopped**
- **1 teaspoon salt**
- **Chinese parsley (optional)**
- **Grated ginger (optional)**

Clean chicken. Place in it a large pot with water to cover. Cook on high heat and add ginger, and chung choy. Discard mushroom stems and slice mushroom caps; add to pot with winter melon and pepper. Cook on medium high for 40 minutes. Remove chicken. Add long rice noodles and cook for 10 more minutes or until long rice noodles are translucent. During the cooking time, continuously skim the top of the soup to get rid of fat and scum.

Remove and discard the chung choy. Shred chicken and either add in all chicken meat back into the soup or keep the breast meat whole and make ginger chicken with that. It depends how much chicken you like in the soup.

Add in the green onions and simmer everything together. Add salt. Garnish with Chinese parsley. You can also serve it with grated ginger on the side.

* Nice brand long rice noodles is preferred as it absorbs the soup and tends not to break.

酸辣湯
Hot and Sour Soup
Makes 8 to 10 servings

The long list of ingredients seems daunting, but the combination makes an excellent soup. Hot and Sour Soup became common in Hawai'i only in the last 20 years as it is not Cantonese, but has northern origins.

6 cups chicken broth, fresh or canned
¾ cup lean pork cut into thin strips
6 dried black mushrooms, soaked, stemmed and diced
1 cup spicy pickled turnip (jah choy), rinsed and diced
½ cup slivered bamboo shoots
8 dried cloud ear fungus, soaked, cleaned and sliced
1 container (12 ounces) firm tofu, drained and cut into thin strips or
   ¼-inch dices
½ cup shrimp, deveined and diced
¾ cup cooked chicken, cut into thin strips
8 to 10 drops chili oil or Tabasco® sauce
3 tablespoons Chinese red vinegar or red wine vinegar
1½ tablespoons soy sauce
½ teaspoon freshly ground white pepper
1 tablespoon cornstarch
4 tablespoons water
1 egg, beaten
Salt to taste

Garnishes:
½ teaspoon sesame oil
1 slice ginger root, thinly slivered
2 to 3 stalks green onion, cut into 1½-lengths and slivered

In a large pot, bring the broth to a boil and add pork, mushrooms and pickled turnip. Simmer for 10 minutes. Add bamboo shoots, fungus, tofu, shrimp and chicken. Simmer for another 5 minutes. Add chili oil, vinegar, soy sauce and pepper. Dissolve the cornstarch in water to make slurry and add to soup. Increase heat and cook until soup thickens. While stirring the soup, drizzle in egg and add salt to taste. Remove from heat and pour into serving bowl. Garnish with sesame oil, ginger and green onions.

瑤柱羹
Dried Scallop Soup
Makes 4 servings

his very satisfying classic soup is served all over the world. Because the dried scallops break apart into shreds, they match the slivered bamboo shoots, ham, and long strings of egg perfectly. This soup must be served very hot, in the Cantonese style.

½ cup dried scallops
3 cups cold water
2 cups chicken broth
1 cup bamboo shoots sliced very
    fine (canned or in plastic)
2 eggs, beaten
1 cup ham* minced or sliced very
    fine to match the bamboo shoots
½ cup chopped Chinese parsley,
    reserve a tablespoon for garnish

Soak scallops in cold water for 20 minutes. Drain using sieve and reserve water, but discard any grit. Combine scallops and the reserved water in a pot. Add chicken broth and bamboo shoots; cook on medium heat until scallops are tender, about 30 minutes. Add in the beaten eggs while the soup is boiling. Add ham strips and parsley. Garnish with remaining parsley and serve immediately.

* Salty, smoky Yunnan or Virginia ham
  is preferred.

Keep it Fresh

It's easy to forget how hard life must have been before refrigeration. Every food needed to be eaten immediately or preserved in some way. Methods included sugaring, salting or brining, curing, fermenting, pickling, drying, and smoking. Examples of these methods found today include the sugared vegetables and fruits served during Lunar New Year celebrations: salt fish (ham yu), brined eggs (ham dan), cured pork like Chinese ham (lup yuk), fermented shrimp (ham ha) and tofu (nam yue and dou foo mui), pickled sweet cucumber (cha gwa) or head cabbage (ham choy), dried oysters, smoked duck, and dried scallops.

冬瓜湯
Winter Melon Soup
Makes 20 or more servings

Do you remember the impressive pale green upright winter melon that was carried to the table and contained the magical combination of savory broth with the sweetness of the melon? In fancy restaurants like the now-shuttered Lau Yee Chai in Waikīkī, the melon would be carved with an intricate design like a dragon. The artistry would draw gasps of amazement from the table and murmurs of delight once they tasted the hot soup. Here is a recipe so you can make this heritage soup for your family in two batches. First the impressive soup in the melon, the second a diced winter melon soup using the top of the melon that couldn't fit in the steaming pot.

> **1 large (10 pound) winter melon (doong gwa), at least 10 inches tall**
> **Large piece cheesecloth***
> **8 cups chicken broth, fresh or canned**
> **6 dried black mushrooms, soaked in 1 cup hot water, stemmed and**
> **diced, liquid saved**
> **1 can (15 ounces) bamboo shoots, diced**
> **⅛ cup dried scallops, soaked in water, liquid saved**
> **1 salted turnip (chung choy), rinsed and minced**
> **1 cup diced raw chicken**
> **½ cup diced Virginia ham***
> **Water in pot for steaming**
> **1 can (14 ounces) gingko nuts**
> **½ cup frozen peas, defrosted**
> **1 egg, beaten**
> **Garnishes: chopped green onions and Chinese parsley**

Wash melon and cut off top, making sure that the melon will fit in your largest stock pot. If you cut more than 3 inches off the top, keep that for the second batch of soup. Scoop out seeds and discard. Place in a large heat-resistant glass or ceramic bowl. Put a large piece of cheesecloth on the bottom of the bowl as a "net" to pull out the melon when soup is done. Place melon on the cheesecloth. Make sure you are able to close the lid of the pot or cut the melon. Place half of the broth, mushrooms, bamboo shoots,

(continued on page 30)

scallops (retain liquid), chung choy, chicken, and ham in the melon. Peel and chop the top of the melon into ½-inch cubes.

In another pot, add these cubes and the rest of the ingredients. You will have batches of soup: one in the whole melon and one in the second pot. Add water from the soaked scallops if there is room in both the melon and the second pot. Pour water around the melon so there is at least 3 inches of water in the pot for steaming. Cover and cook on medium high heat for 2 hours, checking water level every 30 minutes; add more water in the pot as necessary.

Cook the second pot of soup with the diced melon for at least 1 hour to 1½ hours. Check melon for tenderness, if melon is not yet translucent, steam longer. When melon is tender, add in gingkos, peas and egg, while stirring both soups. The egg should cook in 2 minutes. Do not add peas in earlier as they will change to a gray color and starchy instead of bright green and tender.

Have a large bowl ready to hold the cooked melon, next to the pot. Two people will need to lift the cheesecloth and place the melon into the bowl. It will be hot. You can cut away the cheesecloth. Move to the table. Use a spoon or ladle to serve the soup and also parts of the melon. Garnish with chopped green onions and Chinese parsley if desired.

The second pot of soup can be served for seconds after the first batch of soup is served.

* The cheesecloth enables you to present the soup in the cooked melon at the table. Alternatively, you may just leave the melon in the pot and serve the soup from the pot. That is easier to do, but you won't have the spectacular tableside presentation.

**Salty, smokey Virginia or country ham is most similar to the Chinese salty Yunnan ham, but regular canned ham will do.

雲呑
Won Ton Soup

Based on a recipe from Marietta Chong Eng

Makes about 75 won tons

Marietta says that wrapping and eating won ton (dumplings) have been happy family activities for the Chong Sum Wing family for generations. Youngsters have helped make these, but no one exceeded the speed and expertise of grandmother Apo Wing. The won ton was originally made with pork, but as adults began watching their diets, the recipe was adapted for ground chicken or turkey.

Gau Gee Style

Won tons:
- 1 pound ground chicken or turkey
- ½ pound shrimp, peeled, deveined, and diced
- 6 dried black mushrooms, soaked, and sliced
- ½ cup chopped green onions
- ½ cup chopped Chinese parsley
- 1 tablespoon sesame oil
- 1 tablespoon soy sauce
- ¼ teaspoon black or white ground pepper
- 1 chung choy (dried turnip), rinsed and minced (optional)

- 1 pound won ton wrappers or skin (won ton pei)
- Rice bowl full of water

In a mixing bowl, mix together ground chicken, shrimp, mushrooms, green onions, Chinese parsley, sesame oil, soy sauce, pepper, and chung choy, if using.

Folding the dumplings into rectangles or gau gee style:

This is the easiest way to fold. Place a wrapper on your palm and add about 1 teaspoon filling or more in the middle, like a log. Dampen the edges of one side with water, fold the wrapper over and press around the edges to seal. This style is usually fried.

(continued on the next page)

Cap or boat style:

Spread one won ton skin on your palm with point towards the wrist and add 1 teaspoon of filling in the center. Fold into a triangle. Dip a spoon handle in the water and wet the left top corner. Take the two side points of the triangle and twist them together so the corners rest on top of each other, resembling a hat.

Cook the won ton in boiling water for a few minutes until dumplings float to the surface and meat is cooked. Option: add noodles and it becomes Won Ton Mein. Boil noodles separately and serve won ton and noodles in a bowl with your choice of toppings.

Soup:
Chicken broth

Optional toppings:
Chopped green onions
Chinese parsley
Sliced char siu
Bok choy, blanched
Won bok, blanched
Shrimp, cooked
Snow peas, blanched

Note: Won tons are easily frozen. Layer on parchment or waxed paper without touching. Freeze for at least 30 minutes. They will be individually frozen and now can be put together in a plastic bag in the freezer. Instead of serving won ton in soup, deep-fry and serve with hot mustard and soy sauce or sweet chili sauce.

雞肉白菜薑湯
Chicken Napa Cabbage Ginger Soup

From Tiffany Yajima and Loretta Luke Yajima
Makes 6 servings

Napa cabbage is widely used in Asian cuisines. This sweet, crunchy cabbage originated near Beijing, China. Tiffany fondly remembers her mother, Loretta making this soup.

1 whole chicken
½ cup Hawaiian rock salt, divided
1 tablespoon garlic salt
1 teaspoon ground black pepper
1 to 2 fingers ginger (to taste), peeled and sliced
1 head Napa cabbage (won bok)

Clean chicken. Keep neck and gizzard for soup. Other innards can be discarded or used for another dish. With a palm full of the rock salt, thoroughly rub the outside of the chicken cavity. Repeat inside the chicken. Sprinkle the chicken with garlic salt and ground black pepper.* Place chicken, chicken neck and gizzard in a slow cooker and fill with water to cover. Add ginger slices, set on low and leave to cook overnight, 10 to 12 hours.

The next day, remove the chicken and set aside. Transfer the soup stock to a pot and strain the broth to remove any small bones. Skim off any oil or if you have the time, cool and refrigerate. After cooling, the oil will be easy to remove. Clean and chop won bok and add to soup. Heat on high until won bok is barely soft. Serve chicken on the side or add it to the soup. Enjoy with your loved ones and serve with hot rice.

* Tiffany suggests that you get a helper to apply the seasonings as you rotate the chicken.

中式火鍋以及配料

Chinese Hot Pot Soup
and Dipping Sauces

Based on a recipe from Jean Tsou Tsukamoto

Makes 12 servings

When you want to have a party where guests cook what food they like, a hot pot is the answer. This is a fun way to entertain with a cooking vessel in the middle of the table. Guests select what they would like to eat and have various dipping sauces. Typically, noodles or rice are served at the end of the meal with the soup broth made tasty from all the vegetables and proteins. In Australia, this is called Steam Boat and the Japanese version is called Shabu Shabu.

Soup base:
    1 tablespoon vegetable oil
    3 to 4 cloves garlic, smashed
    8 cups chicken or fish stock
    Shrimp shells (save shrimp shells and freeze them for this broth)

Heat garlic and oil in stock pot. Add shrimp shells and stir until shells become slightly brown and fragrant. Add stock and simmer for 1 hour. Strain shells and retain soup for dipping sauce and for hot pot.

Ingredients to cook in soup:
    1 pound shrimp, peeled and deveined (keep shells to flavor soup broth)
    1 pound scallops
    1 pound squid
    1 pound salmon (sashimi grade, center cut)
    1 pound beef rib eye (very thinly sliced or bought as shabu shabu cut)
    1 pound chicken
    1 container firm tofu (20 ounces), cut into large cubes and/or dried
        tofu sticks (foo jook), soaked and cut into 2 x 1 x 1-inch pieces
    1 pound Napa cabbage (won bok)
    8 ounces watercress or spinach
    12 eggs, in shell for guests to break in the soup
    6 black mushrooms, soaked, stems removed and cut in half
    1 cup green onions cut in 2-inch lengths

(continued on the next page)

1 package dried long rice (12 ounces)
  (pre-soaked), saimin noodles, or
  rice, to serve at the end with
  the broth
Other ingredients you can
  select include: beef tripe,
  cooked until tender, sliced pork,
  chicken livers, pork liver, pork kidney,
  thinly sliced lamb, beef tongue, crab, lobster,
  white fish fillets, fish cake, raw or already cooked
  chicken, fish or beef balls, tatsoi, bean sprouts, choy sum, baby
  bok choy, dried tofu (foo jook)

In a portable cooker, heat the soup broth. Surround the cooker with plates of the various ingredients and bowls for each guest. Make sure you have many chopsticks or tongs so people can put ingredients in the broth and take out the delicacies easily. Watch the level of the soup as you may need to add additional broth as it evaporates. At the end of the night, add the type of noodle or rice you would like to serve.

Tip: To cut the meats thinly, it is easier if they are frozen and easiest if you buy them already thinly sliced!

Better Bean Sprouts

In Hong Kong, women at the open market pinch off the heads and the tails of bean sprouts to make them more elegant, and sell them for a higher price. At fancier restaurants, it's common to have a stir-fry of vegetables with bean sprouts like match sticks—no heads or tails in sight!

Dipping Sauce #1
Yields approximately 1 cup
- ¼ cup hot pot soup stock, heated
- ⅓ cup peanut butter, chunky or creamy
- ½ cup Bull Head brand barbecue sauce*
- 2 teaspoons dark soy sauce
- 2 teaspoons brown sugar
- 2 teaspooons sesame seed oil
- 2 teaspoons Chinese red vinegar
- ½ to 1 teaspoon XO sauce or chili sauce (as desired for spice)
- ½ cup finely chopped green onions
- ½ cup finely chopped Chinese parsley

Melt peanut butter in hot soup; add remaining ingredients except green onions and Chinese parsley and stir until peanut butter melts thoroughly. Cover and microwave slightly as needed.

After sauce cools to room temperature, adjust thickness of sauce with additional soup as desired.

Sauce can be served in individual small (Chinese soup) bowls topped with green onions and Chinese parsley as desired.

* Product of Taiwan, available in Chinese markets. The sauce has a layer of oil on top; include or drain oil as desired.

Dipping Sauce #2 *(for 12 individual sauce containers)*
Yields approximately 1 cup
- ⅔ cup light soy sauce
- 6 tablespoons cooking oil
- 1 tablespoon finely minced ginger
- 2 tablespoons finely chopped green onion
- 2 tablespoons coarsely chopped Chinese parsley

Heat soy sauce and oil in a pot until boiling. Add ginger and green onions and cool. Pour into individual dishes and add chopped parsley.

Dipping Sauce #3 *(for 12 individual sauce containers)*
- ⅔ cup Chinese red vinegar
- ½ cup finely slivered ginger
- Chopped fresh red hot chili peppers (optional)

Mix the vinegar and ginger together and serve in individual sauce containers. Offer chopped chilis to those who prefer them.

雞酒
Chicken Soup with Ginger and Whiskey

From Lorna Lo

Makes 8 servings

This strong soup (called gai jow) is traditionally given to new mothers to start their milk flowing. I'm not sure if it is the strong ginger flavor or the liquor that is the cause, but drink this and you'll start perspiring! This is a favorite soup to have when you are sick.

3 pounds chicken, whole or parts
5 small dried black mushrooms, soaked in hot water for 30 minutes
1 ounce dried wood ear fungus, soaked in hot water for 30 minutes
2 teaspoons oil
4-inch piece ginger, peeled and cut into 4 pieces lengthwise
4 Chinese dried red dates (hung jo)
6 cups water
2 tablespoons salt
1 cup liquor, any type will do, but usually bourbon or Scotch whiskey is used

Clean chicken and cut it into pieces. The traditional size is about 1-inch pieces of chicken. Cut the stems off mushrooms and thinly slice. Clean fungus and cut off any hard parts. Set aside. In a large pot, heat the oil and add the ginger for 2 minutes. Then, still on high heat, add the chicken and stir-fry until the chicken is slightly brown, about 5 minutes. Add dates, water, salt, liquor, mushrooms and fungus to the pot. Bring mixture to a boil, then reduce heat to simmer and cook for 50 minutes. Skim oil and serve hot.

西洋菜湯
Watercress and Pork Soup

From Becky Choy based on a recipe from her grandmother, Fong She Young
Makes 6 to 8 servings

Becky makes this soup often, as watercress is one of the few vegetables that her granddaughter, Sierra Kehrwieder, will eat. Any cut of pork can be used, but Becky's mother said the backbone and tail yield the most tasty soup. You could also substitute chicken or beef.

2 to 3 pounds pork back bone with tail, cut into 1-inch segments
5 bunches watercress, medium sized stems preferred
½ cup soy sauce
1 tablespoon sugar
1 thumb-sized ginger, peeled and smashed
4 quarts water
Hawaiian salt to taste
Chicken broth if needed

Wash the soup bones. Place bones in a large bowl and add soy sauc, sugar and ginger. Marinate at least 20 minutes. Cut about 1 inch off the watercress stems and discard. Cut watercress into 1-inch segments. Put in a large bowl of water and wash well, discarding any yellow leaves.

In large pot, combine pork and its marinade with water; bring to a boil. Reduce heat to low and simmer for 1 hour. Add watercress, salt and cook on medium-low heat until watercress becomes limp. Add chicken broth or additional water, if needed. Do not overcook watercress. Serve hot.

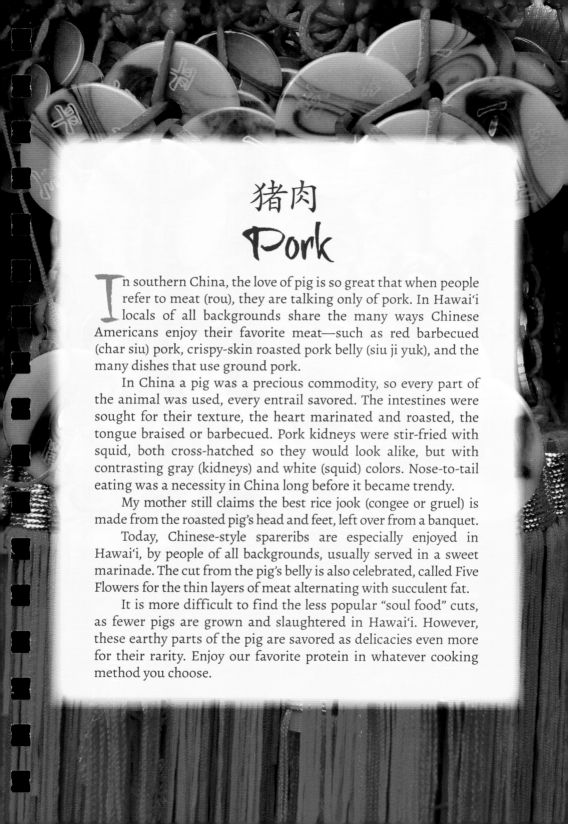

猪肉
Pork

In southern China, the love of pig is so great that when people refer to meat (rou), they are talking only of pork. In Hawai'i locals of all backgrounds share the many ways Chinese Americans enjoy their favorite meat—such as red barbecued (char siu) pork, crispy-skin roasted pork belly (siu ji yuk), and the many dishes that use ground pork.

In China a pig was a precious commodity, so every part of the animal was used, every entrail savored. The intestines were sought for their texture, the heart marinated and roasted, the tongue braised or barbecued. Pork kidneys were stir-fried with squid, both cross-hatched so they would look alike, but with contrasting gray (kidneys) and white (squid) colors. Nose-to-tail eating was a necessity in China long before it became trendy.

My mother still claims the best rice jook (congee or gruel) is made from the roasted pig's head and feet, left over from a banquet.

Today, Chinese-style spareribs are especially enjoyed in Hawai'i, by people of all backgrounds, usually served in a sweet marinade. The cut from the pig's belly is also celebrated, called Five Flowers for the thin layers of meat alternating with succulent fat.

It is more difficult to find the less popular "soul food" cuts, as fewer pigs are grown and slaughtered in Hawai'i. However, these earthy parts of the pig are savored as delicacies even more for their rarity. Enjoy our favorite protein in whatever cooking method you choose.

酸甜排骨
Sweet and Sour Pork Spareribs

From Barbara Ching

Makes about 12 to 14 servings

**4 pounds pork spareribs, cut into
    1-inch pieces**
4 tablespoons cornstarch
3 tablespoons soy sauce
1½ teaspoons salt
**10 tablespoons brown sugar,
    divided**
¼ cup vegetable or peanut oil
**1-inch piece ginger, peeled and
    sliced**
2 cloves garlic, crushed
**1 cup vinegar, or more to taste as
    desired**
1¼ cups pineapple juice
**2½ cups broken pieces Chinese
    slab sugar (wong tong)**
1 tablespoon dry sherry

Patti's Chinese Kitchen

For many in Hawai'i, the quintessential Chinese plate lunch was available at Ala Moana Center at Patti's Chinese Kitchen. You could order the Princess Plate: choice of a starch (steamed white rice, fried rice, chow mein or chow fun) and two selections. If it was a Wednesday, you could get the watercress with roast pork in ham ha sauce (fermented shrimp paste). On Sundays, it was lemon chicken. If you weren't as adventurous, you'd get sweet-and-sour pork or spareribs, beef broccoli, or ginger chicken. The Chun family made Chinese food very accessible.

Clean any bone chips from ribs. In a bowl, marinate the spareribs with a mixture of cornstarch, soy sauce, salt and 2 tablespoons brown sugar for at least 30 minutes. In a large pot or Dutch oven, fry the spareribs in hot oil on high heat until ribs are browned, about 10 minutes.

Add the ginger, garlic, vinegar, pineapple juice, remaining brown sugar, Chinese sugar and sherry. Taste and add more vinegar, if needed. Simmer until ribs are tender, about 45 minutes. Serve.

菠蘿古老肉
Sweet and Sour Spareribs
with Pineapple and Green Pepper

From Lorna Lo

Makes 12 servings or more

P ineapple is the usual pairing with spareribs, but if you're looking for ways to vary it, substitute canned or fresh lychee, mandarin oranges, or rambutan.

4 pounds pork ribs cut into 1-inch pieces
9 tablespoons cornstarch, divided
Peanut or vegetable oil to fry spareribs
2 cups apple cider vinegar
1 cup soy sauce
½ cup Shaoxing wine or any type of liquor
2½ cups brown sugar
1 tablespoon rock salt
5 to 6 cloves garlic, minced
2-inch piece ginger, grated
Juice from 1 can (20 ounces) pineapple chunks,
**   drained and reserved**
1 large onion, cut into 1-inch pieces
1 green bell pepper, cut into 1-inch pieces
4 tablespoons cornstarch
6 tablespoons water
Garnishes: Chinese parsley or chopped green onions

Wash ribs to make sure bone chips are removed. Coat ribs in 5 table-spoons cornstarch. In a pot or skillet, fry ribs on high heat (about 400°F) until brown. Drain and set aside. In a bowl, mix vinegar, soy sauce, wine, brown sugar, salt, garlic, ginger and juice from the canned pineapple. Drain excess oil from pot. Sauté onions, peppers and canned pineapple chunks in pot. Add vinegar mixture and cook on medium heat. Add in ribs and simmer for 1 hour. Do not overcook. Mix 4 tablespoons corn-starch with 6 tablespoons water until dissolved and add to pot. Stir until thickened. Garnish with Chinese parsley or chopped green onions.

叉燒
Char Siu
Chinese Barbecued Pork

From Lillian Carmen Hung Eio Lee Chu
Makes 4 to 5 pounds

Auntie Lil was a great cook. She relocated to California in the 1960s and opened a restaurant on Winchester Avenue in San Jose called Manchu's. Sons Cecil Jr. ("J.R.") and Clayton served as cooks. The popular restaurant offered what American diners wanted, including Chinese sweet roast pork (called char siu), egg foo young, fried rice, fried gau gee, beef broccoli, chow mein and sweet-sour pork.

Char siu paste:
¼ cup ground brown bean sauce (min see jeong)
½ cup hoisin sauce
6 cups sugar
¼ cup salt
1 tablespoon curing salt*

4 to 5 pounds of pork belly, pork shoulder, pork butt or spareribs

Mix bean sauce, hoisin, sugar, salt and curing salt into a paste. Cut the pork into 1 x 2 x 10-inch pieces. Rub paste into the pork and marinate overnight or two nights in the refrigerator. The salts will draw out the moisture from the pork so the paste will seem more like a sauce. Place on a rack and over a foil-lined pan that can hold the dripping oil. Oven roast at 300°F for about 45 minutes to 1 hour, depending on the cut of meat. Cook longer if needed, until pork is tender. Slice and serve or use for other dishes.

Tongue

In Chinatown recently I bought 2 pounds of char siu and discovered that they had marinated and roasted a pig tongue in the char siu sauce along with the normal cut of meat. The texture was firmer than normal pork. I think I'll try to make that one day and serve it as a pūpū: Char Siu Pork Tongue.

* A mixture of table salt and sodium nitrate that you can purchase premixed at most grocery stores.

叉燒五花腩肉
Char Siu Pork Belly
Makes 4 servings

*A*ll over the world, Chinese-themed restaurants serve char siu, but few versions are as sweet or as red as the offerings in Hawai'i. In Hong Kong, I was served thin slices of char siu that melted in my mouth. Surprise. They used the more expensive and fattier pork belly, and more fat always means more flavor and tenderness. The thin morsels were coated with honey, slightly brown, black-tinged on top—but no trace of artificial red coloring. Dark soy sauce and hoisin sauce seem to bring out that brownish-red hue. Here is a recipe that duplicates this style of Hong Kong char siu.

1 pound pork belly with skin, large piece if possible, but strips suffice*

Marinade:
   2 tablespoons Chinese rice wine or dry sherry
   2 tablespoons Chinese dark soy sauce or regular soy sauce
   2 tablespoons dark brown sugar
   2 tablespoons hoisin sauce
   1 tablespoon grated fresh ginger
   2 cloves garlic, minced finely
   ½ teaspoon Chinese five-spice powder
   2 tablespoons honey

Garnish: chopped Chinese parsley (optional)

Wash pork. Cut off skin (freeze for another use); cut meat into 1½-inch strips. Mix marinade ingredients, pour over meat and marinate overnight or for two nights in the refrigerator.

Heat oven to 325°F. Lift pork pieces and let marinade drip off. Oil the baking rack. Place a pan of water on the lowest baking rack to catch the dripping oil from the meat. Discard excess marinade from meat and place on a rack. Brush with honey. Roast about 45 minutes. Halfway, turn meat over and brush again with honey. Test for doneness. If not brown enough for your taste, broil on high for 2 to 3 minutes. Cool at least 10 minutes. Cut against the grain into strips. Garnish with Chinese parsley.

* This cut of pork is called Five Flowers in Chinese. The cuts have five layers of fat alternating with meat.

叉燒排骨
Char Siu Spareribs

Adapted from Cooking the P. Lau Way by Priscilla Lau
Makes 12 servings

In Hawai'i, one of the favorite ways to marinate meat is in char siu sauce. The fundamental ingredients are sweetener, salt, liquor, and Chinese five-spice powder, which is usually made from cloves, cinnamon, fennel, star anise, and pepper. Some versions include ginger or Sichuan peppercorns.

5 to 10 pounds of pork ribs (any type: baby back, center cut, rib tips)

Marinade:
- **2 cups dark brown sugar or Chinese slab sugar**
- **3 tablespoons rock salt**
- **1 teaspoon Chinese five-spice powder**
- **1 finger-sized piece fresh ginger, peeled and roughly grated**
- **¼ cup soy sauce**
- **¼ cup liquor (any type will do, such as bourbon, whiskey or sherry)**
- **¼ teaspoon red food coloring**
- **1½ tablespoons honey**

Garnishes: chopped green onions and Chinese parsley (optional)

Trim fat and silver skin off ribs. Mix marinade together and pour over ribs, but reserve ¼ cup of the marinade for later. Marinate in the refrigerator at least overnight. Rotate the ribs so the meat gets in contact with the marinade.

Grill on the barbecue over a very low fire, preferably over indirect heat. Or bake or roast in the oven at 300°F for 45 to 90 minutes depending on the thickness of the ribs. Best to place ribs on a rack such as an oven rack over a foil lined pan covered with at least ¼ inch of water. This moisturizes the baking and makes for easy clean up. Oil the rack (or use an oil spray) so clean-up is easier. Cover the ribs with foil with holes in it. Bake covered for 45 minutes, then uncover the ribs and brush with marinade. Bake for 15 more minutes or until meat pulls away from the bone. Cut ribs and serve. Garnish with green onions, Chinese parsley or anything green to showcase the red pork.

Note: You can also use this marinade with chicken, pork chops, pork shoulder or pork butt.

燒豬肉
Crispy Skin Roast Pork
Adapted from Donna Woo's recipe
Makes 20 servings or more

I never thought it possible to make crispy skin roast pork at home that would be just as good as what you can buy in Chinatown. Then Carolyn Luke told me about Donna Woo's recipe for crispy skin roast pork (called siu ji yuk), which is every bit as delicious. You do need to buy slab pork belly, but this recipe is easy and quite foolproof.

1 slab (3- to 4-pound) pork belly with skin (about 10 x 10 inches)
2 tablespoons Hawaiian rock salt
2 teaspoons brown sugar
1 teaspoon Chinese five-spice powder
1 teaspoon baking soda (more if the slab is larger)
2 tablespoons canola or sesame oil
Green onions and steamed buns
  (optional)

Clean the pork belly to remove any hair and imperfections. Combine salt, sugar and five-spice powder. The day before you want to eat the pork, coat the underside (meat side, not skin side) with the dry rub. Put a thin layer of baking soda on the skin. Refrigerate overnight uncovered. If you don't have room in your refrigerator for the full slab, lay plastic wrap on both sides of the pork, roll it up and place on a tray, as it will leak due to the brine.

The next day, take the pork out of the refrigerator an hour before roasting to bring to room temperature. Place on a flat roasting rack with foil covering the bottom of the pan to make clean up easier. Preheat oven to 450°F. Wet a paper towel and wipe off the baking

No Leftovers

Our family rarely has leftover roast pork, but if yours does, there are so many ways to use it. Serve it as the protein in fried rice, with taro (see Taro with Roast Pork recipe on page 159) or—my favorite way— steamed with fermented shrimp paste (ham ha).

In a heat-resistant bowl, mix 1 tablespoon ham ha, 1 teaspoon sugar and about 3 cups diced roast pork. Steam 30 minutes. Top with minced green onions and Chinese parsley. I think there is a law that says you must eat ham ha ji yuk (fermented shrimp paste roast pork) with lots of hot rice. **WARNING:** Because of the smell, my mother is wary about cooking this dish now that she lives in a condo. It is as tasty as it is smelly.

soda from the skin. Puncture the skin with a meat tenderizer or poke holes in the skin with a knife. Rub oil over the skin and lay as flat as possible.* Roast skin side up for 1 hour and 20 minutes or until skin is "blistered." Cool before chopping. Serve with a sweeter sauce like plum or hoisin sauce or with hot mustard and soy sauce.

Crispy skin roast pork is also served in steamed buns with sliced green onions as a variation.

* Carolyn's son-in-law, Dane Teruya, inserts three or four metal BBQ skewers through the middle of the pork belly before putting it in the oven to keep it even and this somehow prevents shrinkage.

豆豉排骨
Black Bean Spareribs
Makes 4 servings

The Hakka Chinese love salted black beans to flavor pork. Some feel that black bean spareribs (called *dau see pai gwat*) taste even better the second day.

1½ tablespoons dried salted black beans (dau see), rinsed and smashed
1 tablespoon soy sauce
1 tablespoon cornstarch
1 teaspoon kosher salt
1 teaspoon Shaoxing wine, dry sherry or liquor
2 teaspoons sugar
2 cloves garlic, minced
½-inch piece ginger, minced
1 pound pork spareribs (pai gwat), cut into 1-inch pieces
Garnishes: chopped green onions and chopped Chinese parsley

Mix all ingredients except pork and onions in a heat-resistant ceramic or glass bowl. Add spareribs and mix so the marinade coats the pork. Put in a steamer and steam on high for 1½ hours or until the pork is tender. Or, simmer for 45 to 60 minutes, until tender. Skim oil. Garnish with green onions or Chinese parsley and serve hot.

椒鹽豬排
Pepper Salt Pork Chops

From Keoni Chang, corporate chef at Foodland
Makes 4 to 5 servings

he combination of pork chops and the spicy flavoring make this dish one of the most ordered at restaurants. Adjust the seasonings to your taste and treat your family.

5 thin-cut pork chops
⅛ teaspoon garlic salt
1 teaspoon soy sauce
2 tablespoons sherry
¼ cup flour
¾ cup cornstarch
1 teaspoon ground white (or black) pepper
2¼ teaspoons fine salt (not iodized), divided
2 cups vegetable oil
1 red jalapeño pepper, cut into ¹⁄₁₆-inch slices
2 stalks green onions, cleaned and chopped ⅛-inch
Garnishes: chopped green onions or sliced red jalapeño peppers (optional)

Marinate the pork chops in the garlic salt, soy sauce and sherry for 20 minutes at room temperature.

In a large bowl, mix together flour, cornstarch, white pepper, and ¼ teaspoon of the fine salt.

In a wok, heat the oil on medium high until it reaches 350°F. When oil is ready, dredge each pork chop in the flour mixture and slowly place 2 of the pork chops in the hot oil. Fry them until golden brown on both sides and done, about 5 to 10 minutes.

Once all the pork chops are cooked through, remove them with a slotted spatula and place them on a plate lined with paper towels to drain. Continue cooking the remaining pork chops. After the pork is cooked, remove all of the oil from the wok and reserve the oil. Wipe the wok clean of excess flour. Add back 2 tablespoons of oil and heat on high. When the oil is hot, add the jalapeño peppers, remaining 2 teaspoons salt and green onions; stir-fry 1 minute, then return the pork chops to the wok, gently stir to coat the chops and let them cook for additional 1 to 2 minutes. Remove to serving platter; garnish and serve.

魷魚蒸肉餅
Steamed Pork Hash with Dried Squid

From Susu Markham's mother, Sylvia Lee Leong

Makes 6 servings as a main dish, or more as part of a multi-course meal

½ piece chung choy (dried, salted turnip)
1 dried squid (about the size of your hand)
1 pound ground pork
1 egg, beaten
1 clove garlic, minced
⅓ can (8 ounce) water chestnuts, minced
1 teaspoon sugar
½ teaspoon salt
1 tablespoon cornstarch
1 tablespoon soy sauce
1 tablespoon white wine

Soak chung choy and dried squid separately in water for at least 30 minutes. Drain and chop both into ⅛-inch pieces. Mix all ingredients together into a large Chinese ceramic bowl. Press the pork mixture around the bowl until the sides have more of the mixture than the center of the bowl. Steam for 30 minutes or until set in the middle and fully cooked. Serve hot.

Variations:

- Omit dried squid and sugar. Add in whites of 2 salted eggs (ham dan, see recipe on page 110) to the pork. Top mixture with the two yolks and steam.

- Omit squid and sugar. Add a piece of salt fish (ham yu) that has been soaked in water for 30 minutes to the top of the pork hash and steam.

燒肉
Kau Yuk with Taro
Chinese Pot Roast Pork
Makes about 10 servings, 2 to 3 bowls

This Chinese pot roast pork (called *kau yuk*) is better than the type served in restaurants as it is leaner, more flavorful and has no food coloring. I have fond memories of my maternal grandfather, John Sau Lee, who would steam this in a large Chinese bowl, then turn it upside down so all the pork skin was on top. The staging of the pork and taro, pork then taro, upside down, fascinated me. In Zhongshan, China, the kau yuk with taro that was served in 2014 was identical to what Goong Goong used to make.

4 pounds lean pork belly
¼ cup Chinese red thick soy sauce (hung see yau)*, divided
1 tablespoon vegetable oil
5 pieces fermented red bean curd (nam yue, not the chili bean curd)
2 teaspoons five-spice powder
3 tablespoons brown sugar
2 teaspoons rock salt
½ cup water
2 pounds Chinese taro (woo tau)**, peeled and cut into 2 x 2 x ½-inch
**   slices to match the size of the pork slices**
Steamed buns (optional)
Chopped Chinese parsley and green onions (optional)

Clean pork if needed. Cut pork belly into 4 x 4-inch chunks. Boil in water for 20 minutes to soften, drain and rub with 2 tablespoons soy sauce all around. In a sauce pan on high heat, put oil and brown the pork. Keep turning so it doesn't burn.

Cut into ½-inch strips so it looks like think bacon slices. Coat in 1 tablespoon soy sauce. Brown again for color.

Mix together bean curd, five-spice, sugar, salt, water, and remaining soy sauce and pour over the pork in the sauce pan. Cover and simmer pork for 10 minutes on medium heat.

In a large Chinese bowl, alternate vertically pork/taro/pork/taro/pork taro with the skin side down. Will make 2 to 3 bowls depending on the size of your bowls.

Pour sauce over pork/taro. Place in steamer and steam for 2 to 2½ hours or until pork and taro are tender. Drain liquid and skim off fat.

Flip into a larger bowl, add the liquid and top with parsley and green onions for garnish.

Serve hot as is, or with steamed buns.

* Use regular soy sauce if you cannot find the red, thick soy sauce.

** If you can't find Chinese taro, use Hawaiian taro or white salad potatoes, what Goong Goong would call "Irish Potatoes."

木須肉
Mu Shu Pork
Shredded Pork and Vegetables
Makes 4 to 6 servings

I n this recipe, pork may be substituted with shrimp, chicken or firm fried tofu.

½ pound pork butt, sliced very thin
2 tablespoons soy sauce, divided
2 tablespoons Shaoxing wine or
    sherry
1 teaspoon cornstarch
2 tablespoons oil
1 teaspoon grated ginger
2 tablespoons onion sliced thin
2 eggs, beaten
½ pound spinach or won bok
1 cup dried lily flower (gum choy),
    soaked in water
1 cup cloud ear fungus, soaked in water
½ teaspoon salt
1½ teaspoon sugar

Green Onion Brushes

A fun way to serve green onions is to make them like brushes that can be used to spread the hoisin sauce on the pancakes/flatbread. Using the white end of the green onion, cut pieces into 1½-inch lengths. Using a sharp knife, cut the ends of the green onion about ¼-inch down, in a cross-hatch pattern. Place in ice water and the ends will "bloom" and will look like a brush.

Serve with:
    Mandarin Pancakes (see recipe on page 13)
    ½ cup hoisin sauce and slivered green onions

Marinate the pork slivers in 1 tablespoon soy sauce, wine and corn-starch for 5 minutes.

In a wok or skillet, heat oil on medium high. Brown ginger and onions in hot oil, then add in marinated meat. Stir-fry until brown, about 3 minutes. Remove. Scramble eggs in skillet and stir until cooked. Break eggs into small pieces and set aside. In a small pot, parboil spinach. Drain and squeeze out water. Cut off hard ends from lily flower and cut in half. Cut hard ends off cloud ears and slice into thin shreds. Add spinach, lily flower and fungus into meat mixture.

Add eggs, salt, remaining soy sauce, sugar and spinach. Cook for a few more minutes. Serve on a platter along with Mandarin Pancakes (see recipe on page 13), hoisin sauce, and green onions.

獅子頭
Lion's Head
Makes 6 servings

When this popular dish from Shanghai is served, the large meatballs resemble a lion's head; the cooked won bok cabbage, a flowing mane. The sweetness of the cabbage goes well with the mild meatballs.

3 dried black mushrooms
1 pound ground pork
1 small onion, chopped
2 teaspoons dark soy sauce
2 teaspoons light soy sauce
2 tablespoons Shaoxing wine or dry sherry
1 teaspoon salt
1½ teaspoons sugar
½ teaspoon white pepper
1 tablespoon grated ginger
3 tablespoons vegetable oil
1 head Napa cabbage (won bok), washed and cut lengthwise
    into 8 wedges with core attached
1½ cups chicken broth
Garnish: chopped green onions

Soak dried mushrooms in hot water for at least 30 minutes. Discard stems and mince. In a large bowl, mix together pork, onion, both soy sauces, wine, salt, sugar, pepper and ginger. Divide meat into 6 portions and form into meatballs. In a large skillet, heat oil, then add cabbage and gently stir for 2 minutes. Add broth and place meatballs on top of the cabbage. Cover and cook over medium-high heat for 20 minutes or until meatballs are cooked. Arrange cabbage on platter to resemble a lion's mane and place meatballs on top. Garnish with chopped green onions and serve.

豬腳醋
Sweet and Sour Pig's Feet

From Myrna Ching, through Eldon Ching
Makes 2 feet

This delicious dish is said to help new mothers recover from childbirth, but all visitors get to enjoy it when they visit the home. Some scientific benefit is likely, as the vinegar is said to draw calcium from the bones into the broth. Supposedly the vinegar also helps the uterus contract back to normal size.

When selecting pig's feet for this dish, the meatiest pieces are not considered the best. The front legs have more gelatin and tendon, making for meat with a chewy texture.

My aunt, Cecilia Wei Lo, made this often, even without the excuse of someone having a baby!

2 pig's feet, cleaned and cut into 2-inch pieces if the butcher will do so
3 quarts water
1½ cups rice wine vinegar
1½ cups Chinese black vinegar
1½ cups water
2 cups dark brown sugar
5-inch piece ginger, peeled and sliced

Clean feet. In a large pot, parboil pig's feet in 3 quarts of water for 20 minutes. Drain. Add feet with vinegars, 1½ cups water, sugar, and ginger; cook 1 to 1½ hours, or until tender.

Some recipes call for boiling eggs, peeling them, then adding them in the sweet and sour broth for the last 30 minutes.

Wash Your Meats

Contemporary Americans are rarely exposed to the animals that provide our meats. This distance from the source means that people may be shocked to see nipples on the skin of pork belly or feathers still in a chicken. We forget, are simply unaware, or choose to forget, that a sterile piece of meat wrapped in plastic came from an organic, and sometimes unsanitary, actual animal.

Thus, the first step in many Chinese recipes, even if it's not specifically mentioned, is to wash your ingredients thoroughly. Wash poultry in water, and if it is especially dirty use coarse rock salt as the scrubbing agent. When using cut pork spareribs, it's especially necessary to wash away any bone chips.

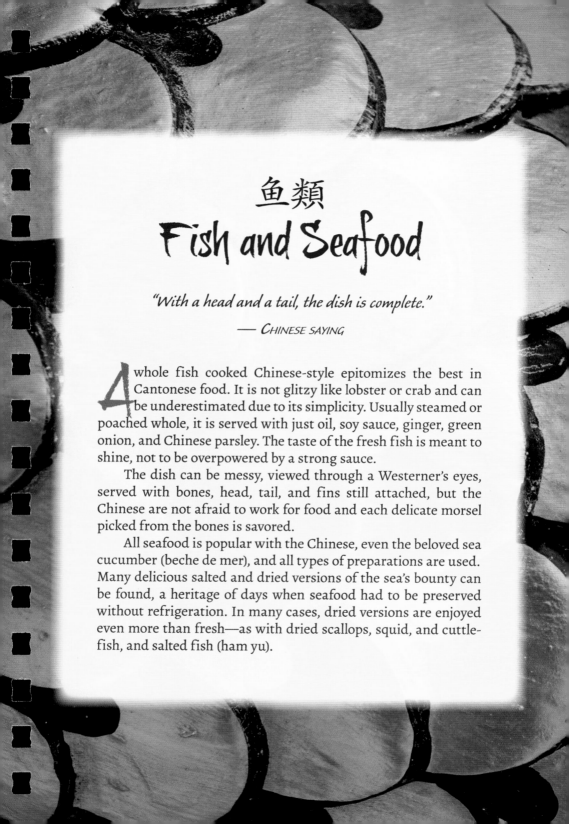

鱼類
Fish and Seafood

"With a head and a tail, the dish is complete."

— CHINESE SAYING

A whole fish cooked Chinese-style epitomizes the best in Cantonese food. It is not glitzy like lobster or crab and can be underestimated due to its simplicity. Usually steamed or poached whole, it is served with just oil, soy sauce, ginger, green onion, and Chinese parsley. The taste of the fresh fish is meant to shine, not to be overpowered by a strong sauce.

The dish can be messy, viewed through a Westerner's eyes, served with bones, head, tail, and fins still attached, but the Chinese are not afraid to work for food and each delicate morsel picked from the bones is savored.

All seafood is popular with the Chinese, even the beloved sea cucumber (beche de mer), and all types of preparations are used. Many delicious salted and dried versions of the sea's bounty can be found, a heritage of days when seafood had to be preserved without refrigeration. In many cases, dried versions are enjoyed even more than fresh—as with dried scallops, squid, and cuttlefish, and salted fish (ham yu).

清蒸全魚 (清蒸海上鮮)
Chinese-style Poached Whole Fish
Makes 6 servings

Iknow that many people steam their whole fish, but try gentle poaching instead. It produces a very delicate texture and allows a more generous window for perfect results.

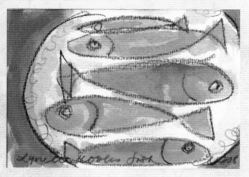

With steaming, the fish can overcook if left to steam too long. This is how my mom, Lorna Lo, does it, and at gatherings everyone seems to go for the fish first.

In the '60s, my Auntie Diana Lee was dating Lloyd Komagome. At first, my grandfather wasn't too keen on that, as he would have preferred a Chinese son-in-law. But my Uncle Lloyd is a fisherman and would catch kumu, which Goong Goong loved to cook Chinese-style. We can't say it was the only reason, but those fishing skills might have been the deciding factor in Goong Goong's approving the marriage.

> 1 whole fish (moi, kumu, mullet, toau, 'ōpakapaka. Usually these fish result in the soft texture that is wanted here, what my mother's family calls "waht." Second choice of fish, since they will have a more meaty texture: salmon, uhu, snapper). This could mean a 2½-pound 'ōpakapaka or 2 to 3 one-pound mullets
> 6 inches ginger, peeled, sliced and divided
> ½ cup slivered or chopped green onions
> ¼ cup chopped Chinese parsley
> Water to cover fish
> ½ cup peanut or vegetable oil
> ¼ cup soy sauce

Clean the fish. Even if the fish market does it for you, it may not be a complete job. Crunching on a missed fish scale takes away from the enjoyment of the dish. Feel the fish and remove any scales. My mother even uses good scissors and cuts off the fins so the fish fits in the pot better and no one gets cut from the fins.

(continued on the next page)

Peel the ginger. Cut the older, tougher part into slices and put in the pot with water (this is the pot where you will cook the fish). The ginger can sit in the water all day as the flavor of the ginger cuts the "fishiness" of the fish. Use a large, covered pot that will fit the fish. A fish poacher is best if you have one. Cut the younger part of the ginger into slivers as fine as you can and set aside. Chop or sliver green onions. Chop Chinese parsley.

Take the fish out of the refrigerator about one hour before cooking to bring it to room temperature. About 40 minutes before you want to serve the fish, place ginger and water into a large pot that will fit the fish. Estimate the amount of water you will need to cover the fish. Bring to a boil.

When the water reaches a boil, turn off the heat and put the fish in the water and cover to seal. In about 20 minutes the fish will be done, unless you are cooking a huge fish, like two five-pound uhu (parrotfish), in which case, you may want to leave the water on simmer (instead of turning the heat off) for 20 minutes.

To check the fish, cut with a knife or fork and look at the color near the bone. Drain fish (discarding water and large slices of ginger) and put on a platter that has enough room for the sauce. Top fish with ginger slivers, green onions and parsley. In a small sauce pan, heat the peanut or vegetable oil. Test to see if it is hot enough by dropping in a piece of green onion. If it sizzles, it is hot enough.

Pour hot oil over the ginger, green onions and Chinese parsley. The oil will cook the greens and ginger and season the oil. Quickly add soy sauce to the same pot. This will heat up the soy sauce. Pour the soy sauce over the fish. Serve immediately and enjoy.

Guest of Honor

Protocol calls for the whole fish to be served with the head facing the guest of honor at the dinner.

清蒸魚片
Steamed Fish Fillets

From Xiao Mei Miu

Makes 2 servings

When faced with a time crunch, this could be a tasty, healthy solution —a quick and easy meal.

8 ounces white fish fillet, whole or in several pieces
2-inch piece ginger, peeled, sliced and slivered into thin
  matchsticks
1 tablespoon chopped green onion
½ teaspoon sherry
2 teaspoons light soy sauce
2 teaspoons peanut or vegetable oil

Place fish fillet on a heat-resistant plate or bowl that will fit in a steamer. Add ginger, green onion, sherry, soy sauce and oil over fish. Steam fish on high for about 7 to 9 minutes (depending on the thickness of the fillet). Remove from steamer and serve immediately.

自製魚餅
ʻŌʻio Fish Cake from Scratch
From Lloyd Komagome
Makes about 3 cups

O ne can only imagine how many fish have been thrown back into the ocean because they had too many bones. The person who invented fish cake was ingenious.

2 cups ʻōʻio (bonefish), scraped from the bones*
½ cup cornstarch
1 cup chicken broth
1½ teaspoons salt

Using a teaspoon, scrape fish meat from the bones. Place the scraped ʻōʻio in a large mixing bowl. Add cornstarch and chicken broth; mix slowly at first with a spoon. Remove any fish bones. Add salt and you can mix a bit faster as the fish absorbs the broth and cornstarch, until it reaches the firmness you want. Use as you would store-bought raw fish cake.

* Awa awa (ladyfish) is another local fish that is often used for fish cake

Fish Cake Appetizers
Makes about 50 to 60 pieces

A t parties, these appetizers are the first to be eaten. Fried foods are always delicious and the soft texture of the fish cake is a nice contrast with the crispy vegetables.

3 cups raw Chinese fish cake
¼ white or yellow onion, chopped
1 celery stalk, chopped
1 tablespoon oyster sauce
2 cups vegetable oil for frying

Mix the fish cake with the onions, celery and oyster sauce. In a wok or skillet, add oil to pan fry or deep-fry. When oil is hot, dip a small spoon into water (to keep the fish cake from sticking) and scoop the fish cake mix into the oil. Cook 2 to 7 minutes on each side or until golden brown. Serve warm or at room temperature.

春花卷
Fish Cake Egg Rolls
Makes 10 servings

This was one of the prettiest dishes that Popo would serve. The thin yellow of the egg crêpe contrasts with the fish cake, mushroom, and green onion filling, and the spiral design was attractive.

6 eggs, divided
3 tablespoons cornstarch
4 tablespoons room temperature water
2 tablespoons vegetable oil
1 pound raw Chinese fish cake
1 can (8 ounces) water chestnuts, minced
4 green onions, minced
½ teaspoon sesame oil
½-inch piece ginger, minced
1 teaspoon soy sauce
5 black mushrooms, soaked, stemmed and minced
Garnishes: green onions and Chinese parsley (optional)

Mix together eggs, cornstarch and water. In a small sauce pan, heat a small amount of the oil and cook 6 thin egg crêpes. Alternatively, if dividing into six portions is too difficult, individually mix 1 egg with 1 teaspoon cornstarch and 2 teaspoons water and mix each crêpe separately. Set aside.

Mix fish cake, water chestnuts, onions, sesame oil, ginger, soy sauce and mushrooms. Spread a thin layer fish cake mixture on each egg "crêpe" and roll like a jelly roll. Place on a plate or shallow bowl and steam for 10 to 15 minutes until fish cake is cooked. Slice into ½-inch pieces and put on a serving platter. Garnish with green onions and Chinese parsley.

Sometimes Popo would make a thin gravy to top these egg-fish cake rolls by mixing oyster sauce (about 2 tablespoons) with a cornstarch slurry (2 tablespoons cornstarch with 4 tablespoons water). Heat mixture until cornstarch has thickened and pour over the cut fish cake rolls.

生魚沙律
Raw Fish Salad

Makes 8 to 10 servings as a first course

This salad is not served as often as it was when I was a child. That's surprising, since raw fish is so popular in our state. Perhaps people prefer the simplicity of making poke or sashimi. But this is a spectacular dish, its textures and pickled favors in perfect balance. This dish is often made in San Francisco, where they use "hard head" fish—striped or black bass.

2 ounces rice sticks (pai mai fun)
Vegetable oil to fry rice sticks
1 head iceberg lettuce, washed, drained and shredded
1 cup turnip peeled, julienne cut and squeezed dry
1 cup carrots peeled, juliene cut and squeezed dry
1½ pounds firm, raw white fish (sashimi-grade), such as pāpio (trevally or jack cravelly), nairagi (striped marlin) or kajiki (blue marlin), mahimahi (dorado or dolphin fish), sliced thinly
2 tablespoons soy sauce
2 tablespoons vegetable oil
½ teaspoon sesame oil, divided
1 tablespoon fresh lemon juice
¼ teaspoon ground white pepper
1 cup green onions sliced thinly, divided
½ cup julienned sweet pickled cucumber (cha gwa)*
½ cup julienned pickled white ginger
¼ cup julienned pickled red ginger
1 tablespoon brown sugar
½ teaspoon dry hot mustard
¼ teaspoon Chinese five-spice powder
Juice of 3 lemons
1 cup Chinese parsley, chopped
1 cup peanuts roasted and chopped
2 tablespoons toasted sesame seeds
Garnishes: parsley, sesame seeds, julienned pickled ginger, fried rice sticks, etc. (optional)

(continued on page 68)

Fish and Seafood

Fry dried rice sticks in hot oil until fluffy, white, and crunchy. Break into pieces and set aside. Prepare lettuce, turnip and carrots and set aside in refrigerator. Mix fish with soy sauce, vegetable oil, ¼ teaspoon of sesame oil, 1 teaspoon of lemon juice and pepper. Set aside. Mix ½ cup of green onions, cha gwa and gingers together. Put over marinated fish. Mix together brown sugar, hot mustard, five spice, remaining green onions, lemon juice, parsley, peanuts, sesame seeds, remaining sesame oil, and most of the fried rice sticks. Toss all mixtures with lettuce, turnip and carrots. Garnish with remaining fried rice sticks, parsley and sesame seeds. Serve immediately.

* Available at some grocery stores and at all Asian markets.

魚肉釀青椒
Fish Cake Stuffed Peppers

Makes 8 servings as part of a multi-course meal or about 36 appetizers

1 pound raw Chinese fish cake
5 shrimps, peeled, cleaned and chopped
3 stalks green onion, chopped
½ teaspoon finely ground white or black pepper
3 large green or red peppers, washed, seeded and cut into
    1½ x 1½-inch pieces
1 tablespoon vegetable oil
1 tablespoon water

Mix together fish cake, shrimp, onion and pepper. Spoon filling into the peppers. Put oil into a cast iron skillet or saucepan. On medium heat, add stuffed peppers, pepper side down. Reduce heat to low and cover. After 5 minutes, add 1 tablespoon of water and cover. After 20 minutes more, turn over peppers so fish cake side is down. Cover and cook for 5 minutes or until peppers are soft. Add additional water as needed. Remove earlier if you prefer a crunchy pepper. Serve hot or at room temperature.

酥炸蠔士卷
Fried Oyster Rolls

From Rose Fong through her daughter-in-law Grace Fong
and grandson Brian Enoka
Makes 24

It's been more than 40 years since I tasted my popo's oyster rolls. She would fry them, as in this recipe, or steam them and make a light gravy with cornstarch, water, and—of course—oyster sauce!

2 dried oysters, soaked in water overnight in refrigerator
1 pound pork caul fat or fat netting (mong yau)*, soaked in water
2 cans (8 ounces each) oysters or 2 (10-ounce) jars of fresh oyster
**   meat, drained and chopped**
½ can (8 ounces) bamboo shoots, chopped
¼ cup chopped green onions
¼ cup chopped Chinese parsley
¼ cup diced water chestnuts
1½ pounds ground pork
½ cup diced ham
¼ teaspoon pepper
½ teaspoon salt
1 tablespoon cornstarch
2 eggs, beaten
2 cups soda cracker crumbs**
Vegetable or canola oil for deep-frying

Change the water of the dried oysters and boil for 30 minutes. Drain and soak with fresh water. Discard any hard parts of the oyster. Rinse the caul fat in cold water several times to clean. Spread on a cutting board and cut into 2½ x 3-inch pieces. Keep refrigerated until ready to use.

In a large mixing bowl, combine both types of oysters, bamboo shoots, green onions, Chinese parsley, water chestnuts, pork and ham.

Add in pepper, salt and cornstarch. Scoop about half a cup of mixture and mold into a small rounded tube, like the shape of an oyster, about 1 by 2 inches. If you are able to obtain caul fat, wrap the oyster mixture in caul fat. Place in a heat-proof dish or pan. Cover with foil and steam for 30 minutes. Cool. This can be prepared a day ahead and kept in the refrigerator or frozen. Roll in egg, then in cracker crumbs.

(continued on the next page)

Deep-fry in hot oil for about 3 to 5 minutes, or until roll is brown and inside is cooked. Drain on paper towels. Serve hot or at room temperature.

* Omit if you cannot find this, but pan fry the oyster rolls instead of deep-frying as the mong yau holds the oyster roll mixture together.
**May substitute fine panko or bread crumbs.

薑蔥生蠔
Fresh Oysters with Ginger and Green Onion

From Myrna Ching
Makes 10 servings

24 raw oysters
5 tablespoons oil
1½ cup green onions, cut ½-inch in length
2 cloves garlic, sliced
1 tablespoon sliced ginger
4 tablespoons dry sherry
4 tablespoons soy sauce
¼ teaspoon salt
1½ teaspoons sugar

Add oysters to a pot of boiling water and cook for 30 seconds. Remove from pot and drain.

Heat oil in wok or skillet, add green onions, garlic, ginger and fry for a few seconds. Add oysters, sherry, soy sauce, salt and sugar. Stir-fry over high heat quickly. Remove and serve immediately.

椒鹽魷魚
Pepper Salt Calamari

From Kirin Restaurant
Makes 4 servings

½ pound calamari, cleaned and
   cut into 1 x 3-inch pieces
1 cup cornstarch
2 to 3 cups oil, divided
½ cup chopped green onion
2 tablespoons fresh red chili
   peppers, chopped
1 teaspoon **Chinese five-spice**
   powder
¾ teaspoon salt
¼ teaspoon ground white pepper*

Coat each side of the calamari with cornstarch. Deep-fry in oil (reserve 1 tablespoon) until golden brown, about 2 to 3 minutes. Drain on paper towels. In a wok on high heat, add remaining oil. Add onions and peppers for 10 seconds. Do not burn. Add five-spice powder, salt, pepper and calamari and stir for 20 seconds. Serve immediately.

*Kirin buys pepper salt already mixed from Chinatown.

A Feast

Cantonese food can be the least expensive or the most expensive.

Our ancestors from Heong Shan (the former name of the region) were happy to come to Hawai'i and be fed rice and salt fish (ham yu) with vegetables. Look at the inexpensive nature of rice and steamed eggs, a mainstay of early Hawaiian Chinese. At the same time, luxury banquets can be most expensive, as the steamed fish must be fresh—discriminating diners can tell when it's not. Other high-end foods in China include sea cucumber, birds nest, shark's fin and abalone.

豉椒海鮮
Black Bean Seafood

From Lorna Lo

Makes 6 servings as part of a multi-course meal

† he fun of eating crab, lobster and clams is the process of digging through the shells to get all of that sweet seafood. Chinese never consider eating "work."

2 tablepoons vegetable or peanut oil
3 cloves garlic, minced
½ pound ground pork
4 tablespoons Chinese dried black beans, rinsed in ¼ cup hot water
1½ teaspoons soy sauce
1½ teaspoons salt
1 tablespoon sugar
1 tablespoon liquor (bourbon, whiskey, or dry sherry)
3 to 4 pounds lobster or crab cut into 1-inch pieces or clams, shrimp or a combination
3 tablespoons cornstarch mixed with ½ cup chicken broth
½ cup chopped green onions
1 egg, beaten
Garnishes: chopped green onions or Chinese parsley (optional)

In a large skillet, heat pan with 2 tablespoons vegetable or peanut oil. On medium heat, stir-fry the garlic lightly until golden brown; add ground pork and cook until pink color is gone. Drain black beans and smash them and combine with soy sauce, salt, sugar and liquor. Add black bean mixture to pot and cook for 10 minutes on medium-high heat. Add seafood and cook 10 minutes. Add the cornstarch and broth mixture and green onions and cook another 10 minutes. Add in egg and cook about 2 minutes or until egg is cooked as desired. Garnish and serve hot.

炆鮑魚
Abalone Stew

From John Sau Lee
Makes 4 servings

Real abalone is more tender than abalone-like shellfish, but is so expensive now. This was not the case 40 years ago when Goong Goong would prepare this. Substitute abalone-like shellfish.

10 dried black mushrooms, soaked in hot water at least 30 minutes
2 cups water
1 can (8 ounces) sliced water chestnuts
½ can (15 ounces) bamboo shoot tips, julienned
¼ cup oyster sauce
2 teaspoons sugar
2 teaspoons cornstarch dissolved in 2 tablespoons water
1 can (15 ounces) abalone or abalone-like shellfish, thinly sliced, keep juices
Garnish: 3 stalks green onion, sliced or chopped

Discard mushroom stems and cut mushroom caps in half. In a pot, cook mushrooms, water chestnuts and bamboo shoots in water over medium-high heat for 5 minutes. Add oyster sauce, abalone juices and sugar and cook for 2 minutes. Add cornstarch mixture and cook until thickened, for about 4 minutes. Add abalone, stir and remove from heat immediately so abalone does not toughen. Transfer to a serving bowl and garnish with green onions.

蠔士鮑魚炆燒肉
Dried Oyster, Abalone, Roast Pork Chopped Stew

From Becky Choy

Makes 6 servings

This recipe for How See Nup is from Becky's grandmother, Fong She Young, who had 11 children and used to cook in the small kitchen at Young Yung Store at Oahu Market in Honolulu's Chinatown. Becky and her mother, Bernice Young Choy, once organized the tenants to save the market from demolition. How See Nup is one of their family's party dishes.

1 tablespoon oil
1½ pounds Crispy Skin Roast Pork (see recipe on page 48), diced
1 pound dried oysters (should be large and plump)
1 can (15 ounces) abalone or top shell, drained and diced
1 can (5.5 ounces drained weight) whole button mushroom, quartered
1 can (15 ounces) whole bamboo shoots, diced
1 can (14 ounces) gingko nuts
½ cup oyster sauce
3 tablespoons sugar
¼ cup soy sauce
¾ cup water
1 can (14 ounces) chicken broth or fresh chicken broth (optional)

Oahu Market

Soak oysters until soft, for about 1 hour. Remove hard round area in oyster. Cut oyster into ½-inch pieces.

In a large sauce pan heat the oil on medium heat and add roast pork and stir. Add oysters and stir. Add abalone, mushrooms, bamboo shoots, gingko nuts and stir. Add oyster sauce, sugar, soy sauce, and water; simmer on low for 10 minutes. Add chicken broth, if needed.

Serve with hot rice or lettuce leaves.

蜜桃蝦球
Honey Walnut Shrimp

Based on notes from Fook Yuen Restaurant
Makes 4 servings

This dish is a more recent arrival in Hawai'i, yet is very popular. It's a favorite of my sister-in-law, Bunnie Smith Lo, and my nephew, Dane Keoni Lo.

1 pound extra large shrimp, peeled and deveined, tails removed
1 egg white
¼ cup cornstarch
⅛ teaspoon baking soda
⅛ teaspoon salt
⅛ teaspoon ground white pepper
4 cups vegetable oil, divided
2 tablespoons sweetened condensed milk
¼ cup mayonnaise
1 tablespoon lemon juice
½ cup Candied Walnuts (see recipe on opposite page)
Garnish: chopped Chinese parsley (optional)

Dry shrimp on paper towels. In a small bowl, mix together egg white, cornstarch, baking soda, salt, pepper and 1 teaspoon of the vegetable oil. Add shrimp and make sure batter coats shrimp.

In another small bowl, mix condensed milk, mayonnaise and lemon juice. Mix and refrigerate.

In a wok or deep skillet, heat remaining oil. Deep-fry the battered shrimp in batches until golden brown. Remove from oil and drain on paper towels. When all the shrimp is cooked, mix with mayonnaise mixture and display on a platter. Top with candied nuts, garnish with Chinese parsley and serve.

Candied Walnuts

Makes one pound

*M*ake these any time for a great snack.

1 pound shelled walnuts
3 cups water
2 cups sugar
2 cups vegetable oil

In a medium pot, boil water and blanch walnuts. Rub skins off as much as possible. In that same pot, combine 3 cups water and the sugar. Heat until sugar is dissolved. Add walnuts and boil for 5 minutes. Turn off heat and let walnuts soak in the sugar water for at least 3 hours. Drain and let walnuts dry for at least 2 hours or you can bake the walnuts in the oven at 200°F for about 5 minutes.

Heat the vegetable oil and deep-fry the sugared walnuts until they are brown. Drain on paper towels. Be careful not to burn them as they could only take a minute or two to cook. Cool completely before placing into an airtight container or top the Honey Walnut Shrimp on page 76.

咖喱龍蝦配椰糕
Curried Lobster with Fried Haupia

Hilton Hawaiian Village
Makes about 4 servings

Many of us wanted our banquets to be held at the Hilton Hawaiian Village just to eat this famous dish created by Executive Chef Dai Hoy Chang of the Hilton Hawaiian Village's Golden Dragon Restaurant. He improved on the Chinese concept of fried milk to create fried haupia, which is perfect with the sweetness of the lobster in curry sauce.

4 tablespoons vegetable oil, divided
1 small potato, cubed
3 tablespoons diced onion
8 ounces (1½ cups) lobster tail meat, cut into 1½-inch cubes
¼ cup chicken broth
¼ cup curry powder
¼ cup coconut milk
2 tablespoons half & half
Dash of salt and pepper
2 tablespoons cornstarch mixed with 2 tablespoons chicken broth
¼ cup green peas
¼ cup cooked diced carrots
3 tablespoons raisins
Garnish: 8 pieces Deep-Fried Haupia (recipe on page 80)

Heat 2 tablespoons oil in wok, fry potato 2 minutes or until cooked; remove and set aside. Heat wok on high heat, add remaining oil, then reduce heat slightly. Stir-fry onion and lobster 2 minutes or until cooked thoroughly. Add chicken broth, curry powder, coconut milk, half & half, salt, and pepper; stir-fry 1 minute more. Stir the cornstarch mixture into the wok. Add peas, carrots, potato, and raisins; cook additional 2 minutes. Place on serving platter. Garnish with Deep-Fried Haupia.

(continued on the next page)

Fried Haupia

Based on a recipe from Hilton Hawaiian Village
Makes 24 to 32 pieces

*U*se your favorite haupia mix or make from scratch using this recipe and deep-fry after the haupia is set.

1½ cups coconut milk
¾ cup water
⅓ cup sugar
½ cup cornstarch
2 tablespoons cornstarch for dusting
Vegetable oil for deep-frying

Egg wash:
1 egg
1 cup water
1 tablespoon flour

Heat coconut milk in double boiler. Stir together water, sugar and ½ cup cornstarch until smooth; stir into coconut milk and cook over low heat, mixing constantly, until thickened. Increase heat slightly and stir the mixture continuously to prevent burning. Pour mixture into a cake pan, 8 x 8 x 2 inches. Cool until set.

To garnish curried lobster dish, cut haupia into about 32 diamond shapes. Otherwise, cut haupia into 24 squares. Dip each in egg wash, dust with cornstarch and deep-fry 2 minutes in hot oil or until light brown. Drain on absorbent paper. Serve with curried lobster.

Fish and Seafood

雞鴨類
Poultry

hicken and duck are staples in every Chinese home and restaurant. Poached, simmered, boiled, braised, fried, roasted, salted, and barbecued are some of the methods used to enhance the birds' good flavor. In addition, we enjoy other types of poultry, including squab, quail, Cornish hen, pheasant, and goose.

As with our nose-to-tail eating of pigs, every part of the bird is utilized, from chicken feet and duck web to ducks' tongues.

A friend from Taiwan who came to the United States in the 1970s thought he had moved to a very special place, as grocery stores would sell trays of chicken gizzards and livers. In Taiwan, those innards were considered delicacies and you would fight over who in the family would get to eat them.

My aunties lament that today's grocery store chickens are not as tasty as those once raised in everyone's backyards. One theory is that the varieties of chicken have changed and the industrial ways in which they are brought to market have altered their flavor and texture.

To serve roast chicken, duck, Cornish game hen or squab in the Chinese manner, serve it with spiced salt. Heat 1 part five spice in a sauce pan, before it smokes, add 2 parts salt. Cool and serve on the side with roasted poultry.

蔥油雞

Ginger Chicken with Jade Pesto

Makes 6 servings

My paternal grandmother, Louise "Ah Gim" Ho Lo, made this often. We just called it white chicken with ginger sauce. I remember her chopping the chicken into about 1-inch pieces using a heavy Chinese cleaver. In those days the chicken was more flavorful, maybe because the birds were free to roam, or because of the type of feed they were given. My popo served it rare, with the meat still pink close to the bone. She had more confidence than I do now in being able to eat chicken rare, so I cook mine all the way through. A similar tasty sauce is used by many restaurants to accompany fish or tofu. They call it a fancy name, Jade Pesto, rather than Chung Yau Geong Jup.

> **1 whole chicken, 2½ to 3 pounds***
> **Water to cover**
> **1 tablespoon rock or kosher salt**
> **Ice and water to fill a large bowl**
> **2 tablespoons peanut or vegetable oil**
> **Garnish: Chinese parsley sprigs (optional)**

Wash and clean chicken to discard fat and remove any remaining feathers. Fill a large pot with estimated amount of water to cover chicken. Add salt and heat to boil. When water is boiling, hold chicken by the legs and dip the chicken in and out of the water 6 times. I was told this is to temper the skin as when you serve the chicken, you want the skin to remain on the meat without tearing. Submerge the chicken on the 7th count; cover and cook until tender, about 50 minutes on medium high heat. In the sink, fill a large bowl with ice and water. When chicken is done, remove from the pot, saving the broth** and plunge the chicken into the iced water to stop the cooking. Let sit there for 5 minutes. Drain and place on a platter or bowl and rub the chicken skin with oil to keep the skin moist. Cut into serving pieces. Sometimes, my grandmother would serve this chicken with just a small bowl of oyster sauce. The chicken may be served at room temperature or chilled. Garnish with Chinese parsley if you do not cover the chicken with the Jade Pesto (ginger sauce).

(continued on page 84)

Jade Pesto (Ginger Sauce)

½ cup grated or finely minced ginger
½ cup green onions
½ cup Chinese parsley
8 cloves garlic, minced
1 tablespoon salt
½ cup peanut or vegetable oil

In a heat-resistant bowl, add ginger, green onions, Chinese parsley, garlic, and salt. In a small pot, heat remaining oil. When sizzling hot, pour oil over ginger mixture. Serve immediately in a bowl, or pour over chicken. If you refrigerate this sauce, make sure to bring it to room temperature before serving. However, I recommend that you make this right before serving as the smell of the oil in the sauce is quite appetizing and the color is most vibrant.

* Buy the freshest chicken you can find to be able to taste the quality of the bird. If possible, buy local, free-range chicken that has never been frozen. Cook the chicken neck, liver, heart and gizzards with the chicken or freeze for another time such as when you want giblets for turkey stuffing.
**Freeze this broth and use when chicken broth is requested.

臘腸蒸雞
Lup Cheong Chicken
Makes 4 to 6 servings

This is one of our family's favorite dishes. The first variation uses fresh chicken; the second was how my mother would transform the basic, frozen, roasted chicken that she would be forced to purchase in large quantities from Jenny Tom and Ginger Grimes during St. Andrew's Priory fundraisers. I think they used to call those benefit chickens Piopio, since they couldn't legally call them Huli Huli chicken.

Fresh chicken version:
- 1 chicken (about 3½ pounds), cut up
- 1 pound lup cheong (Chinese sausage), cut thinly at a diagonal
- ½ pound fresh mushrooms or soaked dried black mushrooms, sliced and stems removed
- 3 tablespoons soy sauce
- 2 tablespoons sugar
- 2 tablespoons julienned fresh ginger
- 3 cloves garlic, minced
- ½ teaspoon black pepper
- 1 stalk green onions, diced
- ¼ cup chopped Chinese parsley
- 2 tablespoons bourbon or scotch
- Lily flowers (gum choy), soaked, cleaned with hard end removed (optional)
- Garnish: Chinese parsley

Mix all in large bowl. Steam for 1 hour. Mix in a slurry of cornstarch and cold water to the hot broth if you'd like a thicker gravy. Stir for a few minutes to cook the cornstarch. Garnish with Chinese parsley. Serve.

Using pre-cooked chicken:
Cook on medium heat in a large Dutch oven all ingredients except chicken, green onions and Chinese parsley. In about 15 minutes, when lup cheong is almost fully cooked, add cut up chicken and green onions. Cook 10 more minutes. Add water if there isn't enough sauce. Just before serving, mix in Chinese parsley.

Serve with rice (always). Enjoy.

豉油雞
Soy Sauce Chicken

Makes 6 servings

*Y*ou can enjoy this simple recipe every week.

1 fryer cut up or 3½ pounds chicken parts
¾ cup soy sauce
1½ cups water
3 cloves garlic, crushed
1 tablespoon honey
6 star anise
2 tablespoons dry sherry (or other liquor)
2-inch piece fresh ginger, sliced
1 small won bok cabbage
Garnish: chopped green onions

Wash chicken and cut into serving pieces, if using a whole chicken. Combine soy sauce, water, garlic, honey, anise, sherry and ginger in pot and simmer for 2 minutes. Add chicken and simmer for 40 to 60 minutes or until done (test for doneness).

Cut cabbage in half lengthwise, keep the core as it will keep the cabbage together. In a separate pot, simmer the cabbage in salted water until tender, about 15 minutes; drain and cut into 1-inch pieces. Keep the shape of the cabbage and place around a serving platter. Place chicken in the middle of the platter. Skim fat from sauce and pour sauce over the chicken and cabbage. Garnish with green onions. Serve warm.

迷你雞

Minute Chicken

Makes 8 servings

This island favorite is great served with Hawai'i-style Cake Noodles (see recipe on page 140). Pour it over the fried noodles just before serving to keep the noodles crisp.

3 to 4 pounds chicken, cut into bite-sized pieces*
3 tablespoons flour
2 cloves garlic, minced
2 teaspoons minced ginger
½ teaspoon pepper
2 tablespoons sugar
3 tablespoons soy sauce
¼ cup hoisin sauce
2 tablespoons Shaoxing wine or dry sherry
¼ cup vegetable oil
½ cup chopped green onions
½ cup chopped Chinese parsley
1 cup won bok or head cabbage, shredded**

Soak chicken in mixture of flour, garlic, ginger, pepper, sugar, soy sauce, hoisin and wine for at least 1 hour. Heat wok or cast iron skillet until sizzling hot. Add oil and stir-fry chicken in batches at highest heat until brown, then lower to medium heat for 5 minutes. Remove and cook another batch. Toss with green onions and parsley. Serve on a bed of cabbage.

* Using a heavy Chinese cleaver is best with bone-in chicken. Or use boneless, skinless chicken thighs.
**Instead of the shredded cabbage, I often parboil 2 to 3 cups of baby bok choy and mix that in during the last 2 minutes of the chicken cooking. This adds a nice green color to the dish and adds nutrients from the vegetables.

雞絲沙律
Chicken Salad

Based on a recipe from Marian Chuck,
through her daughter, Meredith Ching
Makes 8 servings

2 cups cooked chicken meat (baked, boiled, broiled, etc.), shredded or cut

Marinade:
½ teaspoon sugar
½ teaspoon sesame oil
½ teaspoon salt
1 teaspoon oil
2 tablespoons Chinese red vinegar
2 tablespoons oyster sauce
2 teaspoons soy sauce
1 tablespoon Shaoxing wine or dry sherry

8 cups romaine or iceberg lettuce (about 1 or 1½ heads)
½ to 1 cup celery, julienned or thinly diagonally sliced
½ cup green onions cut in thin strips
¼ cup carrots, julienned (optional)
½ cup toasted slivered almonds
Garnishes: Chinese parsley and crispy won ton strips or chips (optional)

   Mix marinade ingredients and marinate chicken overnight. Toss the lettuce, celery, onions, carrots and almonds with Chinese Salad Dressing or Sesame Salad Dressing (recipes follow on the next page); add chicken. Top with crispy won ton strips or chips just before serving.

Chinese Salad Dressing

Makes about ½ cup

Either salad dressing is great with Mrs. Chuck's Chicken Salad. To make clean up easy, put all ingredients in a jar. Shake and serve.

2 tablespoons sugar
½ teaspoon salt
½ teaspoon black pepper
¼ cup vegetable oil
1 tablespoon sesame oil
3 tablespoons Chinese red vinegar

Mix all ingredients together and chill. It's easy to double the recipe and use it later.

Sesame Salad Dressing

From Janice Ching Yee
Makes about 1½ cups

1 large tablespoon dry hot
   mustard
2 tablespoons water
½ cup soy sauce
½ cup sesame oil
¼ cup peanut or vegetable oil
¼ cup toasted sesame seeds

Dissolve mustard in water. Mix all ingredients together.

House of Hong

One of the best-decorated restaurants in Hawai'i, with its black and red lacquered screens, was the House of Hong on Lewers Street in Waikīkī. We used to say, "It's so beautiful, like the San Francisco restaurants!" It was also known for its unusual chicken salad, which had no lettuce, just mounds of finely sliced celery, crisped in iced water for at least 30 minutes. The Hong family restaurant has closed, but we still remember the food and a special wedding reception held there.

At the 1970 wedding banquet of Diana Lee and Lloyd Komagome at the House of Hong. I'm wondering if we were served the famous House of Hong Chinese Chicken Salad.

樟茶雞
Tea-Smoked Chicken

From Linda Chang Wyrgatsch
Makes 6 servings as a main dish

For many years, Chinese Sichuan peppercorns were illegal to bring into the United States, but now they are sold everywhere. The distinctive smell and taste of the peppers are hallmarks of foods from the Sichuan region. Linda says that every time she serves this chicken she is asked why she doesn't open a restaurant. She also tells me that if you can cook, your husband will never leave!

1 whole uncooked chicken, about 2½ to 3 pounds*
2 tablespoons coarse salt
2 tablespoons Sichuan peppercorns**, coarsely ground
½ cup loose black tea leaves***
½ cup sugar

Wash and clean the chicken. Rub salt and peppercorns on the chicken and refrigerate overnight. The next day, put the chicken in a heat-resistant bowl placed in a steamer. Steam chicken until it is almost cooked, about 30 to 40 minutes over high heat. Refill water as needed. Remove and cool.

Use an old steamer pot as it may get discolored. Place a sheet of foil on the bottom of the pot. Place the tea leaves and sugar on the foil. Place chicken in a heat-resistant bowl in the top part of the steamer. Cover. Turn on to high heat, then reduce the heat to medium. The mixture will burn and cook into a bubbly blackened mess and give out smoke. Let the chicken smoke for 8 to 10 minutes. Cool. Cut into pieces or shred. Serve warm or cold.

If you don't have a steamer, you could use a large, old pot, put the foil on the bottom, add some kind of rack that the chicken can rest on. Punch holes into a disposable foil pie pan so the smoke can get to the chicken. Another alternative is to smoke the chicken in an outdoor stand-alone smoker, still using the sugar and tea to add fragrance.

* Linda often smokes 16 drumsticks instead of a whole chicken.
** Substitute black peppercorns.
*** Linda has used ground coffee instead of tea leaves with good results.

酸甜杏仁扁鴨
Pressed Almond Duck with Sweet and Sour Sauce

From Janice Ching Yee
Makes 6 servings

In the 1960s, I think the most popular way to serve duck in Hawai'i was boneless and pressed. Its crispy goodness is accented with a sweet-sour sauce.

3 to 4 pounds duck
1 tablespoon soy sauce
1 teaspoon salt
1 teaspoon Chinese five-spice powder
½ teaspoon black or white pepper
2 cups cornstarch
1 quart peanut oil for frying
1 tablespoon soy sauce
2 tablespoons ketchup
¾ cup sugar
½ cup cider vinegar
1 can (20 ounces) pineapple chunks, drained (reserve juice)
1 tablespoon cornstarch dissolved in 2 tablespoons pineapple juice
Garnish: ½ cup toasted almond slivers or slices

Cut duck into 4 sections. Marinate duck in soy sauce, salt, five-spice and pepper overnight, or at least 1 hour. Place in bowl and steam for 1 hour. Debone duck and dredge pieces in cornstarch, covering all sides. Deep-fry the duck in hot oil until crisp. Cut into smaller, servable portions.

In a saucepan, mix together soy sauce, ketchup, vinegar, sugar and pineapple juice (less 2 tablespoons) and bring to a boil. Lower the heat to medium. Add cornstarch solution gradually until the sauce is the consistency desired. Add pineapple chunks. Make more cornstarch solution with water if you prefer a thicker sauce. Add sugar and vinegar to taste.

On a serving plate, place duck pieces, cover with sweet and sour sauce. Top with almonds.

薏米填鴨
Barley Duck

Based on a recipe from my maternal grandfather, John Sau Lee
Makes 6 servings or more if part of a multi-course meal

his rich dish is also called *Stuffed Duck* because it is filled with a multitude of delicacies including chestnuts, water chestnuts, gingko nuts, mushrooms, and barley. This was one of Goong Goong's signature dishes; he would serve it cooked so well that the meat was falling off the bone. Although it takes hours to cook, the actual preparation is not time-consuming or complicated.

1 whole roasted Chinese-style duck, cut into fourths*
5 cups chicken broth (homemade or low salt preferred) or water
½ cup duck broth from store (may omit if unavailable)
**1½ dried tangerine peel pieces
(gwo pei or chun pei)**
3 tablespoons oyster sauce
1 cup barley
20 chestnuts, frozen or bottled
**6 dried black mushrooms,
reconstituted**
½ teaspoon white pepper, ground
**1 can (8 ounces) water chestnuts,
rinsed, drained and chopped**
**1 can (15 ounces, drained 8.5
ounces) bamboo shoot tips,
rinsed, drained and chopped**
1 can (14 ounces) gingko nuts, rinsed and drained
Salt to taste
Garnish: Chinese parsley

Peanuts

In China it is customary to place roast or braised duck and chicken over cooked peanuts when serving. The peanuts may be soft or crunchy and some have the slight flavor of five-spice powder, like the boiled peanut recipe on page 7.

Put the duck in the largest covered pot that you have. A Dutch oven is recommended since it will be simmering for hours. Add the chicken broth or water, duck broth (omit oil) if you have any, dried tangerine peel and oyster sauce. Cook, covered, over medium-high heat for 1½ hours, or until duck is very tender and almost falling apart. In another pot over medium-high heat, cook barley in water 30 minutes or until tender; drain. Frozen chestnuts need to be cooked covered or uncovered for about 30 minutes or until tender; drain and cut chestnuts in half. Soak mushrooms in hot water for at least 30 minutes. Save the liquid, in case you would like to add it to the chicken stock or water, but do not use the bottom as it may have grit. Remove stems and dice mushroom caps.

Add pepper, drained barley, mushrooms, canned water chestnuts and bamboo shoots. Cook over medium heat for 20 minutes, uncovered. Add gingko nuts and simmer for 15 more minutes. Add more chicken broth or water or mushroom broth, if needed. Add salt to taste. Remove tangerine peel or mince it and return it to the dish (if you like that unique citrusy taste). Garnish with Chinese parsley and serve.

Silent Thanks

At restaurants in Hong Kong, especially at dim sum houses, you'll see people tap their index and middle fingers, or their three middle fingers on the tabletop. The practice goes back to a Qing Dynasty legend in which an emperor traveling in disguise poured tea for his staff. His attendants were normally required to kowtow or bow, but to do so would have given away the emperor's identity, so he instructed them instead to tap their fingers. The gesture has broadened in meaning to be a general symbol of thanks after someone pours tea or serves food.

* When you buy the roast duck, ask the butcher to cut the duck into quarters.
Ask for duck broth if they have any. To elevate this dish, use FRESH mushrooms, chestnuts, water chestnuts, bamboo shoots and gingko nuts. The next best texture and taste will be to use frozen chestnuts or ginko nuts.

陳皮白果鴨

Duck with Gingko Nut and Dried Orange Peel

Family Recipe from Yen Chun
from her maternal grandparents Wong Lit and Mabel Wong
Makes 6 servings as a main dish, more as part of a multi-course meal

*D*ried orange or tangerine peel (chun pei or gwo pei) is a flavor game changer. Around the world, citrus is used to offset the rich taste of beef and game. In Chinese cookery, it is commonly added to beef or duck dishes that are stewed for hours. The peel adds a distinctive taste and complements the deep flavor of duck or beef brisket or tendon. The peel can sometimes be found at mainstream markets, in the Asian section, but I usually get mine in Chinatown for the best taste. This is a spectacular dish.

1 frozen whole uncooked duck
8 to 10 dried black mushrooms, soaked in 1 cup of hot water for at least 15 minutes, reserve liquid
6 pieces of dried orange peel (gwo or chun pi), soaked in ½ cup of water 30 minutes, reserve liquid
2 tablespoons dark soy sauce*
2 tablespoons rock salt
1 can (14.5 ounces) chicken broth
6 slices peeled ginger
2 tablespoons light soy sauce*
2 tablespoons brown sugar (or a 2 x 1-inch slab of Chinese sugar)
¼ cup Shaoxing wine or dry sherry
1 packet (about 7 ounces) frozen peeled gingko nuts or 1 can (14 ounces with water) gingko nuts
1 tablespoon cornstarch plus 2 tablespoons water
Garnish: chopped green onions

Defrost duck for 2 days in the refrigerator. Soak mushrooms and orange peel in separate bowls of water for at least 30 minutes. Rub duck with dark soy sauce and rock salt. Place in a foil-lined baking pan on a rack, so the oil can drain. Broil on high 10 to 15 minutes on each side until

(continued on the next page)

browned and some of the oil drains. Place duck in a Dutch oven or sauce pan with the chicken broth, liquid from mushrooms and orange peel. Trim stems and slice mushrooms before adding them in with ginger, light soy sauce, brown sugar and wine. Place orange peels on top of duck. Bring to a boil, then reduce to simmer and cover; cook until tender, about 2½ hours. Add gingko nuts after simmering for 1½ hours.

When done, place duck on a serving platter, add the gingko nuts, mushrooms and orange peel around the duck for decoration. To make a gravy from the duck drippings in the pot, skim off oil. On medium heat, stir cornstarch mixture into the sauce and cook until thickened, about 3 minutes. Pour over duck and garnish with sliced green onions.

> ## Cut the Fat
>
> When serving or cooking rich foods, ginger, citrus, turnip or vinegar are used to cut the richness. That is why you'll see tangerine or orange peel (gwo pei or chun pei) cooked with duck, or red vinegar served with noodles cooked with meats or seafood, or pickled ginger served with 1,000-year-old eggs (pei dan). Another example is how often turnip is paired with beef.

* Substitute regular soy sauce if you do not have the dark or light versions. However, it's better if you buy the Chinese dark soy sauce to add color and the light soy sauce to add saltiness.

檸檬雞
Lemon Chicken

Makes about 6 to 8 servings

3 pounds boneless, skinless chicken breast, cut into bite-sized pieces

Marinade:
  1 tablespoon sherry
  1 tablespoon soy sauce
  ½ teaspoon salt

Batter:
  1 egg, beaten
  4 tablespoons water
  ¾ cup cornstarch
  ¼ cup all-purpose flour
  1 teaspoon baking powder

3 cups vegetable or peanut oil

Sauce:
  ⅓ cup sugar
  1 tablespoon cornstarch
  ½ teaspoon salt
  1 cup water or chicken broth
  4 tablespoons fresh lemon juice

Garnishes: Chinese parsley or lemon slices

Two Pots at the Table

In China, and especially Hong Kong, restaurants bring two tea pots to your table: one with tea and one with hot water. Some diners prefer only hot water, others dilute their tea later in the meal, after it has been steeping for a while and has grown stronger. It's a great idea and I wish restaurants in Hawai'i would copy this service.

Combine marinade ingredients and marinate chicken for at least 30 minutes. In a separate bowl, mix egg, water, cornstarch, flour and baking powder together to make a batter.

In a deep skillet or wok, heat oil. In batches, dip chicken in batter and deep-fry the chicken pieces until golden brown. Drain chicken pieces on a plate covered with paper towels. Repeat until all chicken is cooked.

To prepare sauce, mix sugar, cornstarch, salt and broth in a separate skillet or pan and bring to a boil. Then add lemon juice and cook for 1 minute or until sauce thickens.

Place chicken on a serving platter and pour sauce over. Garnish with Chinese parsley or lemon slices.

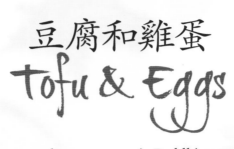

豆腐和雞蛋
Tofu & Eggs

Given bean curd's strong roots in Buddhism and Taoism and its status as the preferred "clean" way of vegetarian eating, it is not surprising that so many tasty Chinese dishes use tofu and other "meat" substitutes.

Wheat gluten (min gun) has been popular in China for centuries. Sold freshly fried and then refrigerated or frozen, or canned with sauces, gluten is added to vegetable dishes as a contrasting texture.

In China, the textures of tofu are much more varied than what is available in the U.S.—you can specify a degree of softness. Dried tofu (foo jook), made from skimming the top of soy bean milk, is available in thicker sticks and sheets, adding a favorite taste and chewy texture.

Although those of us who enjoy tofu can savor it cold and plain, the treatments of braising in sauce, deep-frying and stuffing with meat, are also enjoyed.

Solid forms of tofu include: firm, medium, soft, deep-fried, deep-fried shells (called dau foo pei or aburage in Japanese), dried (foo jook) sticks or sheets, fermented white (dau foo mui), and fermented red (nam yue) tofu. Some versions come with spiced with chili peppers.

Tofu is gaining popularity with the growth of vegetarianism and veganism. Many brands are now available in Hawai'i and throughout the mainland U.S.

Eggs are also a popular protein acceptable to many vegetarians and, like others the world over, the Chinese enjoy their versatility. Many of us remember a simple breakfast, lunch, or dinner of just fried eggs, hot rice, and oyster sauce.

Both duck and chicken eggs are savored fresh or preserved. The most common method of preserving eggs is to brine them for 30 to 40 days in salted water. The eggs—duck or chicken—are then boiled (often in rice while it is cooking). The salted yolk may be used as a strong flavoring, enjoyed in joong or as a topping for vegetables.

Preservation taken to the extreme produces 1,000-year-old eggs, among the most terrifying of foods for their black-gray yolk and translucent topaz-colored "white." The eggs are actually chemically preserved for weeks. Those of us who enjoy their distinctive taste crave them as an appetizer, served with oyster sauce and pickled scallions.

Fresh chicken eggs are beaten and then gently steamed for one of the simplest "peasant foods" ever. Steamed eggs are also economical, but add dried scallops or fresh clams and the steamed eggs become gourmet.

蒸釀豆腐
Steamed Stuffed Tofu

Makes about 10 triangle-shaped pieces

In Zhongshan and Hong Kong, I discovered what they called a Hakka-style dish of stuffed tofu—a 2 x 2 x ½-inch square of tofu with just a smidgen of fish cake, shrimp or ground pork in the middle. The meat stuffing is inserted using the ends of two chopsticks, then the tofu is sprinkled with five-spice powder, powdered chicken seasoning, salt and pepper. It's all fried in a bit of oil.

The version we are familiar with in Hawai'i is a triangle of tofu. It is steamed and heavy on the stuffing.

**1 large block (21 ounces) firm tofu, drained at least an hour with a
plate used as a weight
1 pound raw Chinese fish cake
5 shrimps, peeled and chopped
4 ounces (about ½ of a can) water chestnuts, chopped
2 stalks green onions, minced
Garnishes: green onions and Chinese parsley**

Cut drained tofu into 1 x 3-inch triangles. Slice the middle, where you want to put the stuffing. Mix fish cake, shrimp, water chestnuts and green onions together. Stuff each tofu and steam for 15 minutes, or until fish cake is white. Garnish and serve hot or at room temperature.

蝦米豆腐
Cold Tofu with Dried Shrimp
Makes 6 servings as an appetizer

*O*nce you try this, you'll see how easy and delicious it is. The flavorful shrimp spice up the bland but soothing cold tofu.

1 container (20 ounces) soft tofu (dau foo)
¼ cup dried shrimp, of any size (ha mai)
1 teaspoon sesame oil
2 tablespoons soy sauce
1 teaspoon grated ginger
3 stalks green onions, minced
Garnishes: Chinese parsley and sesame seeds (optional)

Put tofu into a serving bowl for at least 30 minutes. Keep draining the water from the tofu. Soak the dried shrimp in a separate bowl with hot water for at least 30 minutes or until soft. Drain (reserve the liquid if you want to use it as a seasoning for cooked vegetables or add to a soup) and clean shrimp to remove any remaining shells or black innards. Mince as finely as you can. Top the drained tofu with shrimp, sesame oil, soy sauce, ginger and green onions. Serve immediately.

涼拌腐竹
Tossed Foo Jook Salad

From Yan Shiling "Linda"
Makes 8 servings, as an appetizer

This is a very refreshing way to eat dried tofu (called foo jook). It can be served as a side dish or an appetizer. Foo jook is made by skimming the top of the liquid while cooking soy beans to make tofu or soymilk. This healthy byproduct is shaped into sheets or sticks and frozen or dried.

1 bag (6 ounces) dried foo jook sticks (use fresh if available)
Cold water to soak foo jook
6 cups hot water
1 cup chopped Chinese parsley
½ cup finely-slivered carrot
2 teaspoon sesame oil
1 teaspoon salt
½ teaspoon chicken seasoning powder*
1 fresh Chinese chili pepper, finely slivered **
1 tablespoon Chinese red vinegar (optional)

If using dried foo jook, soak the dried sticks in cold water overnight. Drain. Cut into 1-inch pieces and put into a colander. Boil 6 cups of water and pour over foo jook. Drain. Squeeze out all water. In a bowl, mix foo jook with parsley, carrots, sesame oil, salt, chicken seasoning powder and chili pepper. Add vinegar, if desired. Serve immediately or refrigerate and serve cold.

Note: In this tasty salad, we use both the leaves and the stems of Chinese parsley.

* Chicken seasoning powder is used often in current Chinese cooking. It does contain MSG, so if you are sensitive, omit it or substitute ½ teaspoon fish sauce.
** This pepper is not very spicy. If you cannot find it, substitute ⅛ cup of red jalapeño or red bell pepper, finely slivered.

麻婆豆腐
Ma Po Dou Foo
Spicy Cooked Tofu
Makes 4 servings

This famous dish is supposedly named after the woman who first cooked it. She had a pock-marked face and became famous because of her tofu creation.

2 teaspoons vegetable oil
2 cloves garlic, minced
¾ cup ground pork or ground beef
1 tablespoon hot bean paste*
1 teaspoon soy sauce
1 teaspoon Shaoxing wine or sherry
2 teaspoons sugar
½ cup soup stock or water
1 container (20 ounces) soft tofu,
   drained
1 tablespoon chopped green onion
2 teaspoons cornstarch dissolved in
   2 tablespoons water
½ teaspoon sesame oil
Garnishes: chopped or slivered green onions and Chinese parsley
   (optional)

In a wok or a skillet, heat oil and brown garlic over medium-low heat being careful not to burn the garlic or it will be bitter. Add meat and stir-fry until almost done. Add bean paste, soy sauce, wine, sugar, and soup stock. Bring to a boil; add tofu and green onions. Add cornstarch mixture and cook for 2 more minute or, until mixture is thickened. Add sesame oil, garnish and serve hot.

* If the flavor of bean paste is not to your liking, substitute chili-garlic sauce, sriracha or freshly cut chili peppers.

魚豆腐

Easy Tofu and Gluten

Makes 2 servings

This is a wonderful, fast dish for your vegetarian friends.

> **1 can (10 ounces) fried, flavored gluten, Chai Pow Yu***
> **1 container (20 ounces) firm or soft tofu****
> **½ cup chopped green onions**
> **¼ cup chopped Chinese parsley**

In a pot or skillet, empty the entire can of gluten including the sauce. Add tofu and green onions and heat over medium heat. When heated through, top with Chinese parsley and serve.

* Sometimes called vegetarian mock abalone.
**While this recipe has more tofu than gluten, less tofu can be used.

炸釀豆腐
Mānoa Valley Stuffed Fried Bean Curd

From Sig Zane
Makes 8 to 10 servings

*A*lthough Sig Zane has helped to make Hilo famous, he grew up in Mānoa Valley and named this dish after his first hometown. He created this delicious dish drawing on his Chinese heritage, but added a Korean flair with the kim chee!

4 Chinese black mushrooms, soaked in ¾ cup hot water for at least 30 minutes, reserve liquid
1 salted dried turnip (chung choy), soaked in water for 15 minutes, drained, and minced
1 pound ground pork
1 can (8 ounces) water chestnuts, drained and minced
1 can (15 ounces) bamboo shoots, drained and minced
1 tablespoon oyster sauce
½ teaspoon white pepper
1 teaspoon Hawaiian salt
½ teaspoon grated ginger
½ cup chopped green onions
½ cup chopped Chinese parsley
2 eggs, beaten
½ cup won bok kim chee drained and chopped
About 7 unseasoned fried tofu rectangles
    (called dau foo pei in Cantonese, aburage in Japanese), cut in half diagonally (approximately 0.4 ounce)
2 cups chicken broth, divided
Garnish: chopped Chinese parsley or chopped kim chee (optional)

Drain and mince mushrooms after discarding the stem, but retain liquid. In a large mixing bowl combine and mix together chung choy, pork, water chestnuts, bamboo shoots, oyster sauce, pepper, salt, ginger, green onions, Chinese parsley, eggs, and kim chee; stuff fried tofu shells. Once cut, there is a natural pocket to stuff. You may be able to make 12 to 20 depending on the size of the fried tofu. Place in a heavy pot, with stuffing facing up. Pour the mushroom liquid and 1 cup of the chicken

(continued on the next page)

broth in the pot and turn heat to medium high. After liquid comes to a boil, reduce heat to medium-low, cover and simmer for 1 hour. Add more chicken broth or water to refill the pot after 25 minutes as needed. Serve on a platter and use the reduced broth in pot as gravy. Garnish with Chinese parsley or kim chee to serve.

Tip: I can imagine delicious variations using squeeze-dried tofu, shrimp, crunchy slices of cloud ear fungus and dried squid. Experiment!

海鮮腐皮卷
Shrimp Fried Dried Bean Curd Roll
From Jade Dynasty Seafood Restaurant
Makes 4 rolls

*J*ade Dynasty is known for innovative food. This dish uses the dried bean curd as the wrapper instead of a flour one.

4 pieces dried bean curd sheet (dau foo pei), soaked in water
6 shrimp (41/50 size), peeled and chopped
⅛ teaspoon salt
⅛ teaspoon cornstarch
Dash chicken seasoning powder
Dash sesame oil
2 tablespoons vegetable oil
2 tablespoons Worcestershire sauce as the dipping sauce

Soak dried bean curd sheets in water for at least 20 minutes, or until supple. Cut into 5 x 5-inch pieces. In a small bowl, mix the shrimp, salt and cornstarch together by stirring in one direction for 5 to 6 minutes. Add chicken seasoning powder and sesame oil and mix for 2 minutes. Divide the mixture into 4 equal parts. Put the shrimp mixture on the bean curd sheet and wrap into rectangle shapes about 3 x 1 inches.

Heat oil in a skillet and pan fry bean curd rolls until they are golden. Absorb any excess oil by blotting on paper towels. Cut them in half, serve with a dipping sauce of Worcestershire sauce.

蒸蛋羹
Steamed Eggs

Makes 4 servings as a main course, or more if part of a multi-course meal

What does a Chinese mother make for dinner when there isn't much in the house? Steamed eggs and hot rice. As with the Japanese custard called Chawan Mushi, the charm of this dish lies in the silky texture of the egg custard. The simplest version comprises just eggs and water. This fancier version uses dried shrimp or scallops.

> **¼ cup dried shrimp or dried scallops**
> **3 eggs**
> **1 cup boiled water, cooled to room temperature**
> **2 tablespoons soy sauce, divided**
> **¼ cup chopped green onions**
> **1 tablespoon vegetable oil**

In a small bowl, cover the dried shrimp or scallops with ½ cup of hot water for at least 20 minutes.

In a large Chinese noodle bowl (any heatproof bowl), beat eggs with water from the dried seafood (make sure to omit any grit at the bottom). Add additional water to make 1½ cups. Add 1 tablespoon of soy sauce. Add drained dried seafood and steam on medium-low heat until the egg is set, about 20 minutes.

Add green onions and steam an additional minute. Do not overcook or the texture will not be smooth. Top with remaining soy sauce and oil. Serve with hot rice.

Variation: In place of the shellfish use ½ pound of ground pork or canned clams (use the juices as part of the water). If you want the meat to be mixed through the custard, you'll need to stir it every 5 minutes as it cooks. If you do nothing, the meat will sink to the bottom.

鹹蛋
Salted Eggs

Adapted from *Cooking the P. Lau Way* by Priscilla Lau
Makes 2 ½ dozen eggs

For many people, the word "preserved" is negative. Not to us Chinese! Preserved meats, fish and vegetables are a delicious and integral part of Chinese cookery. The taste of these "salt eggs" or Ham Dan is just perfect, with just the right amount of saltiness.

8 cups water
1½ cups rock salt
¾ teaspoon baking soda
2 teaspoons black tea leaves
1 lemon, seeded and cut into 4 wedges
2½ dozen uncooked duck eggs or extra large chicken eggs*
Waxed paper

In a stock pot over high heat, dissolve the rock salt, baking soda and tea leaves in water. When salt is dissolved, turn off heat and add the lemon wedges. Cool. The tea stains the egg shells tan.

In a non-reactive container like a plastic container with a lid, ladle a lemon wedge and some of the liquid. Fill container with eggs and gradually add liquid and lemon wedges. Crumble waxed paper and place at the top of the container and cover to make sure the eggs are covered with the liquid. Refrigerate for 40 days. Remove from liquid and store in the refrigerator until ready to use, up to 2 months. I'm sure in my grandmother and great-grandmother's day, they would cure the eggs unrefrigerated. My food scientist friend says refrigeration is not needed during the 40 days of curing as the high salt content cures the eggs, but I still cure them in the refrigerator.

The old-fashioned way of cooking the salt eggs is to place them in the pot when you are cooking rice. Peel and enjoy with the hot rice.

Salt egg yolks are also good to mix in pork hash (see recipe on page 53).

* I have had good results from buying local extra large chicken eggs. Duck eggs are harder to find in urban Honolulu, but they result in richer yolks.

皮蛋
Preserved or 1,000-Year-Old Eggs

From Good Chinese Cooking by Grace W. Kwok
Makes 1 dozen eggs

Connoisseurs of 1,000-year-old eggs enjoy them plain with pickled shallots, steamed with fresh eggs, or in jook. In ancient times, duck eggs were covered with a mixture of mud, pine ash, salt, rice hulls, and lime for months to preserve them. Another name is 100-year-old eggs or Pei Dan. Now, caustic soda can be used to cure the eggs.

1 gallon water
76 grams sodium hydroxide (see note)
1 dozen duck or extra large chicken eggs

Pour sodium hydroxide into water that is in an earthenware jar. Submerge the eggs for 3 weeks. Remove from the jar and soak eggs in clear water for 1 week, changing the water several times a day. Peel eggs and enjoy.

 Note: Food-grade sodium hydroxide can be purchased from online stores. BE CAREFUL as the pure chemical is highly corrosive and caustic. Even chemists are extra careful with it because it can cause severe burns. Remember to **add the sodium hydroxide to water, <u>not</u> water to the sodium hydroxide.**

皮蛋韭菜炒蛋
Pei Dan with Chives and Egg

From Sylvianne Yee

Makes 6 to 8 servings

Those thousand-year-old eggs look scary with their gray and black colors, but actually they are mild tasting. Combine them with garlic chives and fresh eggs for a simple, delicious meal.

1 large bunch fresh garlic chives (about 3 cups)
6 preserved eggs (pei dan, see recipe on page 113)*
10 to 12 fresh large eggs
Salt to taste
Black pepper to taste
2 teaspoons cooking oil
Oyster sauce (hau yau)

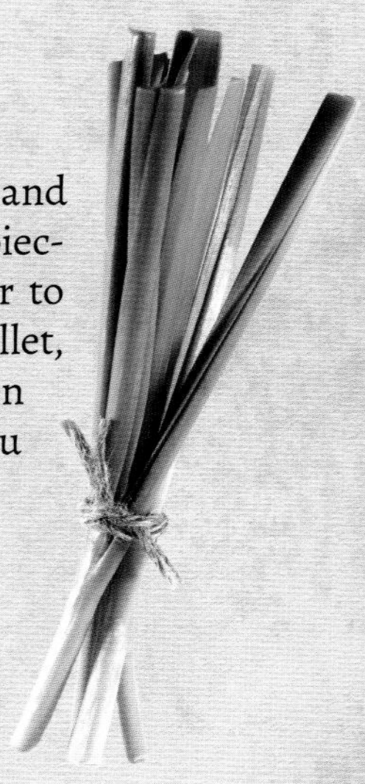

Wash and cut chives into 1-inch lengths. Wash and peel pei dan and cut each egg into wedges (about 16 pieces). Lightly beat the fresh eggs, add salt and pepper to taste, and add pieces of pei dan and set aside. In a skillet, sauté chives in oil until wilted, about 5 minutes, then add mixture of fresh eggs and pei dan. Cook as you would scrambled eggs. Serve with oyster sauce.

Note: Pei dan can also be purchased at Asian stores.

茶葉蛋
Chinese Tea Eggs
Makes 6

tea eggs are beautiful with their dark lines creating a web-like pattern on the white shells. Keep them in the refrigerator as a great snack.

6 eggs
Water to cover eggs
2 teaspoons salt
3 black tea bags or 1 tablespoon loose
    black tea
¼ cup soy sauce
4 star anise
2 cups water to cover eggs

In a small pot, place 6 eggs and water to cover. Heat to a boil, then reduce heat to simmer for 10 minutes. Place pot in sink and run cold water over the eggs for at least 5 minutes. Drain. Gently crack each egg with the back of a spoon, being careful to leave the shell on. Place eggs back in pot with tea leaves, soy sauce, star anise and enough water to cover eggs. Bring to a boil, then reduce heat to simmer for 40 minutes. Cool in the sauce for one hour. You can shell the eggs immediately or upon serving.

牛肉
Beef

Cattle were uncommon in southern China. Pigs were easier to raise on the hilly terrain and on the smaller parcels of land, so traditional beef dishes are few. Cattle's common relative was the water buffalo, used for working the rice fields. By the time the animal could be used for food, it was very, very tough and just about inedible.

In the north, beef was more common, along with mutton (sometimes referred to as goat in the old literature) and lamb.

When found on the Chinese menu, beef was not a main dish, but a type of flavoring. A few ounces could flavor enormous amounts of vegetables or enhance a huge pot of soup.

For stir-fries, Chinese prefer the cut of meat called hanging tender, hanging tenderloin, butcher's steak, or skirt steak (onglet in French). If that is not available, good substitutes include flap meat or flank steak, also called London broil. With all of these cuts, slice the meat across the grain and in uniform pieces. Chinese enjoy every part of the cow, including the tail and the tongue.

番茄牛肉

Beef Tomato

Makes 6 servings

Is this a Chinese dish? Definitely, even though in Hawai'i it is made by almost every ethnic group that it is considered a local dish more than a Chinese one. Traditional Beef Tomato is much like another local favorite, Chopped Steak. If there is any difference, it could be that Beef Tomato has more gravy.

1 pound flank steak, sliced against the grain into about 1½-inch pieces, ¼-inch thin
3 cloves garlic, minced
1 teaspoon Chinese cooking wine or dry sherry
4 teaspoons soy sauce, divided
2 teaspoons cornstarch, divided
4 teaspoons sugar, divided
2 tablespoons vegetable oil, divided
½ teaspoon pepper
1 onion, sliced into slim wedges, with the grain
2 stalks celery, sliced diagonally
1 green bell pepper, cut into wedges
2 tablespoons ketchup
1 teaspoon Worcestershire sauce
3 large tomatoes, cut into wedges
Garnish: Chinese parsley (optional)

Tomato Beef

My husband grew up on the island of Hawai'i, so he calls this Tomato Beef, instead of Beef Tomato. Who knows why people from the Big Island say this? They also say "ice shave" instead of "shave ice." Also, instead of just saying pipe, he says "hose pipe." Hmmm. The mysteries of life.

Marinate the beef with the garlic, wine, 2 teaspoons soy sauce, 1 teaspoon cornstarch, 2 teaspoons sugar and 1 tablespoon oil for 30 minutes.

On high heat, in a cast iron skillet or sauce pan, quickly sauté the beef until it is brown, but not completed cooked. Remove from pan and place in a bowl. In the skillet, add remaining 1 tablespoon of oil and cook the onions, celery and green bell pepper until tender, about 5 minutes. Add the remaining soy sauce, cornstarch, ketchup, sugar, Worcestershire sauce and ¾ cup of water and cook for about 2 minutes, until the gravy is thickened. Add in beef and tomatoes and cook for additional minute. Serve immediately. Garnish with Chinese parsley.

This is also good as a topping for Hawai'i-style Cake Noodle (see recipe on page 140) or Fried Noodles (Chow Mein, see recipe on page 143).

炆牛百葉
Tripe Stew

From Lorna Lo

Makes 12 or more servings

This is probably a "local" recipe, rather than a pure Chinese one, but so many families enjoy this stew. My mother doesn't add potatoes, but I notice that in her father's recipe, he added what he called Irish potatoes. The Hawaiian chili peppers provide a great contrast to the sweetness of the sauce and green peppers.

4 to 5 pounds honeycomb tripe
Water to cover tripe in pot
2 tablespoons rock salt
6 cloves garlic, smashed, divided
2-inch piece ginger, peeled and
  cut into slices, divided
1 tablespoon freshly ground black
  pepper
½ cup soy sauce
½ cup Shaoxing wine, dry sherry
  or liquor
3 slices bacon, cut into ½-inch
  pieces
4 cans (10.5 ounces each) condensed tomato soup
1 can (8 ounces) tomato sauce
2½ cups water
3 bay leaves
2 onions, cut into 1-inch pieces
3 to 5 Hawaiian chili peppers, depending on your preference
3 large green bell peppers, seeded and cut into 1-inch pieces, divided
3 carrots, cut into 1-inch pieces
4 celery stalks, cut into 1-inch pieces
Salt to taste

Special Order

Lorna Lo's granddaughter, Hannah Claire Chan, says, "I 'order' tripe stew from Grandma's Kitchen every time I'm home. It's a cross between a soup and a stew, and I love her tripe stew with that tomato-ey sauce."

(continud on page 120)

Trim fat from tripe and cut into 1 x 2-inch pieces. In a large pot, bring water, salt, 3 cloves garlic and half of the ginger to a boil and parboil the tripe for 20 minutes; drain, rinse, and cool. In a large bowl, combine the remaining garlic, ginger, pepper, soy sauce and liquor; massage cooled tripe with marinade for 5 minutes.

Using the same pot, brown the bacon over medium heat for about 5 minutes. Drain the bacon fat; add tripe and the marinade and simmer over medium heat for 15 minutes. Add tomato soup, tomato sauce and 2½ cups of water*, bay leaves, onions, chili peppers, green peppers (reserve 1 cup of peppers), carrots and celery; cook on medium or low heat until tripe is tender, about 1 to 1½ hours. Test for tenderness every 10 minutes and watch for burning.

Add the remaining green peppers and cook until vegetables are tender, about 10 minutes more. Serve with hot rice or poi and chili pepper water or Tabasco® sauce.

* Do not add additional water until the end. If it is too thin, you'll need to add a cornstarch slurry.

To get every drop of the tomato soup, my mother would always pour the water into the soup cans before pouring the water into the pot.

苦瓜牛肉
Beef with Bitter Melon
Makes 4 servings

You either love bitter melon or you hate it. If you're like me, the bitter taste is very appealing and I want that quinine flavor to be as strong as possible. We can't understand people who blanch the vegetable before cooking to tone down the taste.

3 tablespoons Chinese dried salted black beans (dau see),
    rinsed in ¼ cup of hot water
3 garlic cloves, minced
1-inch piece ginger, minced
1½ teaspoons soy sauce
1½ teaspoons salt
1 tablespoon sugar
1 tablespoon liquor
1 pound flank steak, cut against the grain
    in thin 1 x 2-inch pieces
1 tablespoon peanut or vegetable oil
3 large bitter melons, seeded and cut
    into ¼-inch diagonal slices
3 tablespoons cornstarch mixed with ¼ cup chicken broth or water

Drain the black beans and smash them in a bowl. Add the garlic, ginger, soy sauce, salt, sugar, liquor and meat. Mix together and let sit at least 5 minutes to marinate. In a hot skillet, add oil and stir-fry meat with marinade until almost cooked, about 4 minutes. Remove meat from pan and set aside. Stir-fry bitter melon for about 4 minutes, or until almost tender. Add meat and juices back into pan. Add cornstarch mixture and stir-fry until thickened, about 3 minutes. Serve hot.

蒙古牛肉
Mongolian Beef

Based on a recipe from Mini Garden Restaurant

Makes 4 servings

I *n cookbooks from the 1950s, I've seen recipes that make a sauce for this dish from a combination of ketchup and A-1® Sauce. One can only imagine a cook in a Chinese restaurant trying to figure out a short cut and inventing this mix. Surprisingly, it is very tasty and so easy. It's great for busy weeknight cooking. Serve over hot rice or put over Hawai'i-style Cake Noodles (page 140) or E-mein (page 145).*

1 pound flank steak, sliced against the grain into 1 x 2 x ¼-inch slices
¼ cup ketchup
¼ cup A-1® steak sauce
4 teaspoons vegetable oil, divided
1 large onion, sliced from top to root, about 2 cups
2 Hawaiian chili peppers, smashed
1 small green bell pepper, sliced thinly, about 1 cup
½ teaspoon black pepper
2 cloves garlic, minced
¼ cup water

Marinate the beef with ketchup and steak sauce in a bowl for at least 10 minutes. In a wok or large skillet, heat 2 teaspoons of oil on high. When hot, add onions, 3 kinds of peppers and garlic and toss often while cooking until onions are translucent, about 5 minutes (time will depend on the heat of your skillet). Remove from skillet and set aside in a platter. Add remaining 2 teaspoons of oil to hot skillet and cook marinated beef until desired doneness. Add in vegetables and mix together with ¼ cup of water. Place on platter and serve with hot rice or noodles.

炆牛尾

Oxtail Stew

From Mark Doo

Makes 4 to 5 servings

ark says this "'onolicious" and tender oxtail stew is quite fast and easy to make using a pressure cooker. If you don't have one, though, allow two to three hours of cooking time to ensure the oxtails are tender.

½ cup all-purpose flour
3 pounds oxtail
2 tablespoons canola
  or vegetable oil
1 medium onion, chopped
3 cloves garlic, minced
½ cup red wine (the darker red
  the better)
1 teaspoon salt
1 teaspoon ground black pepper
½ teaspoon red pepper flakes
½ teaspoon Chinese five-spice
  powder
4 cups chicken or beef broth
4 tablespoons butter
4 tablespoons all-purpose flour
1 cup tomato sauce
4 medium carrots, peeled into
  chunks
4 stalks celery, cut into 1-inch
  pieces
Salt and pepper to taste

Pumpkin Bowl

For a unique presentation for oxtail stew, consider a kabocha pumpkin "tureen": Make at least five knife cuts in the top of a kabocha around the stem, outlining a "cover." Microwave 7 minutes. A small pumpkin could cook in this time, but cut open the top and check. If necessary, microwave two minutes more at a time, until done. Remove the seeds and you'll have a container perfect for serving the stew. Scoop out the pumpkin flesh as you serve, as a delicious addition.

Heat the pressure cooker pot over medium high heat. Place flour in a heavy plastic bag or large bowl. Add the oxtails and toss until completed coated. Heat oil in the preheated pressure cooker. Heat until shimmering. Shake off any excess flour from the oxtail then add them to the hot oil. Brown well on all sides without burning, about 10 minutes. Remove from pressure cooker.

The Lee Kwong Family in 1909. Lynette's grandfather, John (Duck) Sau Lee is top row, second from the right.

Reduce heat to medium-low. Add onions and garlic and sauté for 5 minutes, adding more oil if needed. Add red wine and reduce over low heat, until the wine is reduced to half. Use a spoon to scrape the bits of oxtail stuck to pot (this makes the taste).

Add oxtails into the pot with salt, pepper, red pepper flakes, five spice and broth. Add water if the oxtails are not submerged in liquid. Cover pot and bring to pressure. Cook on high for 40 minutes. Turn off heat and let sit for 10 minutes. Melt butter in microwave for about 30 seconds. Add in flour and mix together to make a roux. Release pressure cooker and open according to the manufacturer's directions. Skim excess fat. (Mark's note: remember fat is flavor!) Turn heat to high. When liquid boils, add in butter roux and stir. Add tomato sauce and carrots and celery. Turn down heat and simmer until the vegetables are tender, about 20 minutes. Add additional salt and pepper to taste.

Hilo Chinese Food

Sun Sun Lau was THE place for graduations, wedding banquets, and retirement parties in Hilo. It could seat nearly 1,000 people and was known for its good Cantonese food, such as beef broccoli, fresh noodles, and kau yuk served with 10 white steamed buns (bao) all encased in a single large white bun. The restaurant has closed, but Hawai'i island residents still speak fondly of the place.

Variation: Substitute cinnamon or curry powder for Chinese five-spice powder.

牛肉芥蘭
Beef Broccoli or Chinese Broccoli

Based on a recipe from Mitsuko Saito
through her granddaughter Suzanne Watanabe Lai
Makes 4 servings

his is a delicately flavored Beef Broccoli, made without the commonly used oyster sauce. Serve with hot rice or over Hawai'i-style Cake Noodles (see page 140).

1 cup sliced steak, flank steak or barbecue meat
1 pound broccoli or Chinese broccoli (gai lan)
½ tablespoons fresh ginger juice (grate ginger and squeeze the juice)
2 tablespoons soy sauce
2 teaspoons sugar
2 teaspoons cornstarch
¾ cup water
2 tablespoons salad oil, divided
¼ cup green onions cut into 1-inch lengths

Clean meat and slice diagonally across the grain into 1½ x ½ x ⅛ inches. Wash and clean broccoli, slice into strips ⅛-inch thick. Combine ginger juice with soy sauce and sugar, set aside. Make a smooth paste of cornstarch and 1 tablespoon of water, then gradually stir in remaining water; set aside.

Heat 1 tablespoon of the oil until hot in a wok or skillet. Add beef and stir-fry for a few seconds. Remove meat and set aside in a bowl and add half of the ginger, soy and sugar sauce. Reheat the pan and add 1 tablespoon of oil and stir-fry the broccoli until almost cooked. Add the meat with the remaining sauce, cornstarch mixture and green onions. Bring to a boil and cook until cornstarch is thickened, about 2 to 3 minutes. Serve hot.

炆牛舌

Stewed Beef Tongue

From Lorna Lo
Makes 8 servings

2 beef tongues (about 2 pounds each)
Water to cover
2-inch piece ginger, peeled and cut into rounds
3 cloves garlic, sliced
⅓ cup sherry
½ cup soy sauce
¼ cup peanut or vegetable oil
6 cups water
1 onion, cut into 1-inch cubes
2 star anise
3 carrots, peeled and cut in 1-inch cubes
3 stalks celery, cut into 1-inch lengths
5 inches turnip, peeled and cut in 1-inch cubes
6 white potatoes, quartered
⅔ cup oyster sauce
1 tablespoon kosher salt
⅓ teaspoon ground black pepper
⅓ cup cornstarch dissolved in 1 cup water
1 cup peas, thawed

In a large pot with water to cover, cook the tongues for 1 hour. Then cool in an ice bath* for 20 minutes. With a sharp knife, completely peel off the white coating from the beef tongue. In a large bowl, marinate the tongues with the ginger, garlic, sherry, and soy sauce for 15 minutes.

Heat the oil on high in a Dutch oven. Take the ginger from the marinade and add it to the oil; brown the tongue in hot oil for about 4 minutes on each side. Add the remaining marinade, water, onion and star anise; bring to a boil, then reduce to low and simmer for 1½ hours. Add carrots, celery, turnips, and potatoes and cook for 25 minutes more. Test meat for tenderness. If tender, remove from heat and slice or cube. Skim oil. Add oyster sauce, salt, and pepper. Return meat to the mixture. When vegetables are tender, stir in a cornstarch slurry and cook until thickened, about 5 minutes. Add peas and stir for 2 minutes. Serve hot.

* To make ice bath, fill a large bowl with half ice and half cold water.

飯麵類
Rice and Noodles

Food and rice are so integral to Chinese cuisine and culture that a common greeting is "Have you eaten rice already?"—meaning, "How are you?"

For many, no meal is complete without the favorite starch of the southern Chinese. Fresh-cooked rice is enjoyed one day, then refreshed the next by transforming it into gruel (jook or congee) or mixing it with other leftovers to make fried rice. In Hawai'i, fried rice has become popular with all ethnic groups who incorporate meat in their preparation ranging from Hawai'i's favorite canned meat—Spam®—to Filipino pork adobo to Japanese sausage (arabiki) to Hawaiian kālua pork.

Traditionally, long-grain rice was favored. Today, many have adapted to the medium or short-grain rice preferred by the Japanese. Sweet or glutinous rice is used when a sticky texture is desired, as in the simply delicious No Mai Fan with black mushrooms, Chinese sausage (lup cheong), green onions, and Chinese parsley.

In northern China, wheat, barley, and sorghum are more widespread than rice, so noodles reign.

Our local Chinese meals typically feature both rice and noodles, but it is with noodles that we can see most clearly how a traditional Chinese food has morphed into something distinct—cake noodles. Only in Hawai'i are noodles made as thick, crispy on the outside, soft and sticky on the inside. They are so popular that most restaurants charge more than for the regular Hong Kong-style noodles, which are deep-fried and crispy throughout, or the more common dry fried noodles (gon lo mein). Some children, in fact, just want cake noodles without the pui tow (toppings). Double-fried noodles are popular in China, but nowhere are they made or wanted as thick as we have them in Hawai'i, often cut into squares.

At the noodle store you can specify how you want your noodles—dry, or to serve with gravy, crispy or soft for soup, saimin to make into cake noodles, or a newer favorite—e-mein or e-foo mein (deep-fried at the noodle factory, then dried) that are chewy. Long, uncut noodles are traditionally served at birthday parties to symbolize the wish for a long life.

雞飯
Gai Fan
Chicken Rice
Makes 2 to 3 servings

My popo, Louise Lo, would make this often as a simple, tasty, comforting dish. She would make it in a pot on the stove. An easy version is to use your rice cooker.

1 cup diced chicken, breasts or thighs
½ cup diced bamboo shoots
2 tablespoons soy sauce
1 tablespoon Shaoxing wine or dry sherry
½ teaspoon salt
1-inch piece ginger, peeled and finely minced
2 cups long-grain rice
Water for the rice cooker

Rice in a Pot

It seems old-fashioned to cook rice in a pot when there are so many rice cookers—even high tech varieties. Popo would probably choose a pot even today because of fan jiu—the crusty rice on the bottom of the pot when you make rice in a pot. We used to fight over the crunchy, chewy browned rice.

In a bowl, mix chicken, bamboo shoots, soy sauce, wine, salt and ginger together; set aside. Wash rice and place in rice cooker. Fill water to 2-cup level as indicated on rice pot and start cooker. After 5 minutes, add the chicken mixture to the top of the rice; cover and continue cooking until rice cooker automatically shuts off. Stir and serve.

Variations:

- Substitute lean pork for the chicken.

- Add ½ cup of any type of mushrooms.

醃肉火腿炒飯
Bacon Spam® Fried Rice
Makes 6 servings

*W*hen you're on the mainland, you may find that some people will eat Spam® for the first time when they try your local-style fried rice.

4 cups cooked day-old long-grain rice, cooled (if frozen, at room temperature)
1 tablespoon vegetable oil
2 eggs, beaten
3 strips bacon, cut into ¼-inch strips
1 small onion or half a large onion, diced
2 cloves garlic, minced
½ cup Spam® (or shrimp, ham, chicken, pork, or sausage), cut into ¼-inch cubes
½ cup frozen peas, thawed
3 tablespoons oyster sauce or soy sauce
1 tablespoon sriracha sauce (optional)
¼ cup chopped green onions

It's best to cook the rice the day before if at all possible. Then put the rice in the freezer or refrigerator to dry it out. I like long-grain rice for fried rice as the grains don't stick together as much. However, you can use any type of rice.

In a heated wok or large skillet, add 1 tablespoon vegetable oil over medium heat; scramble the eggs and set aside. In the same skillet, cook the bacon for 4 minutes on medium heat, then add onions and garlic; cook a few more minutes until the onions are translucent.

Add Spam®, rice and peas. Stir-fry continuously until rice separates, about 10 minutes. Add oyster sauce and eggs. Add sriracha sauce if you like a spicy fried rice. Keep stir-frying and make sure that you do not have clumps of white rice. Add green onions, except for a tablespoon, which is used for garnish. Serve hot. Freezes well.

Taro vs. Rice

In 1901, *Ka Lahui Hawai'i*, a Hawaiian-language newspaper lamented that former taro lands are now being planted with rice by the Chinese. It urged Hawaiians to start farming kalo (taro). *Translation courtesy of the Nūpepa Hawai'i blog*

糯米飯
No Mai Fan
Chinese Sticky Rice with Sausage and Mushrooms

From Charlene Lo Chan
based on a recipe from her mother-in-law Ella M. Chan of San Francisco
Serves a crowd of 20 to 30 as a side dish

This is our family's favorite at Thanksgiving. Yes, one more starch in addition to the stuffing, mashed potatoes, and steamed rice. The finely minced meats and mushrooms create a delicious taste and the stickiness of the rice is addicting. It will become your family's favorite, too.

> 1½ pounds dried black mushrooms, soaked, stems removed and diced (results in about 5 cups)
> 2 pounds char siu, diced
> 1½ pounds Chinese sausage (lup cheong), diced*
> ½ cup oyster sauce***
> ¼ cup soy sauce
> 7 cups long-grain rice (you can substitute medium-grain rice)**
> 4 cups sweet rice (mochi rice)
> 10 cups chicken broth
> 4 cups chopped green onions
> 3 cups chopped Chinese parsley, reserve ¼ cup for garnish

Place the diced mushrooms, char siu and lup cheong in separate containers. This can be done the night before. Measure, rinse and drain water from the rice. Keep the two types of rice separated.

Mix the char siu, lup cheong, oyster sauce, and soy sauce together and set aside. In a large pot with a cover, layer the long-grain rice, then mushrooms, then sweet rice. The mushrooms will flavor the long-grain rice when it cooks. Pour in chicken broth until the liquid is about 1 inch above the top of the rice. Cook on high heat until the broth begins to boil, then reduce heat to simmer and cover. When the liquid has been reduced to the top of the sticky rice add meat mixture, cover and continue steaming on low heat until meat is cooked, about 45 minutes. The longer you steam the rice mixture the more flavorful it becomes.

Add additional oyster sauce to taste if you want it sweeter, more soy sauce if you want it saltier. Stir in green onions and Chinese parsley and serve. Sprinkle Chinese parsley on the top before serving.

* Charlene prefers the dried lup cheong sold loose in San Francisco or New York as it is sweeter.
**Everyone has a preference on the stickiness of the rice. One way is 70 percent long-grain rice and 30 percent sweet rice or a 60/40 mix. If you use medium-grain rice combined with the sticky rice, then the mixture becomes much more glutinous.
***She prefers the Lee Kum Kee brand with a woman in a boat on the label.

糯米鸡
No Mai Gai
Sticky Rice with Chicken
From Richard K.C. Lau
Makes 4 servings

This classic dish, No Mai Gai, is sometimes wrapped in lotus leaves or banana leaves and steamed. Richard sometimes adds vegetables. He says to experiment with the flavors you enjoy.

1½ rice-cooker cups sweet rice (mochi rice), rinsed and drained
2½ cups chicken broth, divided
2 tablespoons oyster sauce
2 teaspoons olive or vegetable oil
3 to 4 boneless, skinless chicken thighs, cut into bite-sized pieces
4 to 5 cloves garlic, minced
2-inch piece ginger, peeled and minced
2 Chinese sausages (lup cheong), sliced
4 black mushrooms, soaked, stem removed and quartered
10 dried shrimp, soaked and cut in half
Garnish: Chinese parsley

In a rice cooker, cook rice with chicken broth and oyster sauce to the level of water needed for 1½ cup of rice (about 1½ cup of broth).

In a wok or large skillet, heat oil and fry the chicken with garlic and ginger. Add sausage, mushrooms, and shrimp. Add 1 cup of remaining chicken broth. Add the cooked sticky rice and mix thoroughly. Garnish with Chinese parsley.

糉
Joong
Savory Glutinous Rice "Tamale"

From Rose Fong through grandson Brian Enoka

Makes 25 joong

Joong requires as much prep time as Hawaiian lau lau, so it doesn't make sense to make just one or two. This heavy, sticky rice dish is made savory with pork belly and a rich, salty duck egg yolk. Yum.

5 pounds sweet rice (mochi rice)
⅔ cup short-grain rice
4 pounds pork belly
½ teaspoon Chinese five-spice powder
3 tablespoons Hawaiian salt
25 salted duck or chicken eggs
1 cup raw peanuts, shelled and skinned*
25 or more ti leaves, washed and ribs removed
25 lengths (each 36 inches) kitchen cotton string
⅔ cup Hawaiian rock salt
Water to boil the joong

Traditional Shapes

Most joong (steamed, savory-sweet rice "tamales" with egg and pork) are triangle shaped. Throughout Zhong-shan, I saw cylinder-shaped joong and was told that is the Loong Doo village style. Many in Hawaiʻi are from Loong Doo, so I wonder why that shape did not become common here. Could it be that we are in a time warp in Hawaiʻi and create the foods that our ancestors knew from 160 years ago, when they first immigrated?

The night before you will make joong, wash both types of rice. Mix them together and soak in water. Cut the pork into 25 cubes. Mix pork pieces with five-spice and 3 tablespoons Hawaiian salt. Refrigerate overnight.

The day of cooking, separate the salted egg yolks from the whites and keep in a bowl. You may discard the whites. Drain rice in a colander. Rinse peanuts and mix with rice.

(continued on page 136)

To assemble:

Fold a ti leaf to make a pocket. Scoop about ½ cup of the rice mixture and place half into the ti leaf pocket. Add one egg yolk and one piece of pork. Cover with the other half of the rice mixture (or ¼ cup). Fold the ends of the ti leaf over the rice and tie with a string. It will look like a triangle.

To cook:

Heat a large pot of water. A 20-quart pot will hold about 20 joong so you may need two pots. Add ⅔ cup Hawaiian salt to water in the pot and make sure there is enough water to cover the joong. Cook on a slow boil for 4 to 4½ hours. Add water as needed to keep the joong covered. Cool. Untie the bundle and use the string to cut the joong.

Note: You can freeze joong. To warm it up, put it in boiling water for at least 30 minutes. The texture will not be the same if you microwave it.

Alvin Yee's Traditions

My family's roots are from the See Yup area of Guangdong province. Most local folks are not familiar with that area, but nearly all Chinese immigrants to North America (Hawai'i excluded) prior to the mid 1960s were from See Yup. In the 1970s, I visited Chinatowns in San Francisco, Los Angeles, and Vancouver BC and the language was identical to my parents' dialect. We fold our doong (or joong in Cantonese) differently; Cantonese joong is shaped like a tetrahedron. See Yup doong is elongated with sharp ends that if viewed from the end, the sharp ends are perpendicular to each other. My late mother Wei Sit Tom Yee, originally of Hoi Ping (now known as Kai Ping), instructed me that when cooking joong for 3 hours (simmer only) to place a ceramic spoon inside the pot, and to place a pair of shoes in front of the stove. Don't ask why, just do it.

*   Some families add green mung beans, azuki, or black-eyed peas, instead of peanuts. If you use black-eyed peas, soak them overnight in water. Other families prefer joong without beans. One version also adds a 1-inch piece of Chinese sausage into each joong.

廈門炒米粉
Rice Noodle with Tsin Choy

Based on a recipe for Ha Moon Noodles from Hung Won Restaurant
Makes 4 servings as part of a multi-course meal

T his is one of my favorites, as the pickled mustard cabbage (called tsin choy) makes it very refreshing. Although it includes shrimp and char siu, it doesn't taste heavy. You could make a vegetarian version by substituting black mushrooms and wood ear fungus (chin yee) for the meats.

1 teaspoon peanut or vegetable oil
½ cup slivered pickled mustard cabbage (tsin choy, see recipe on page 155)
¼ cup sliced char siu
¼ cup shrimp, peeled and deveined*
¼ cup slivered green bell paper
¼ cup green onion, cut in 1-inch lengths
¼ cup sliced onion (slice from top to root)
2 eggs, beaten
½ cup bean spouts
1 pound dried rice noodle, soaked for 5 minutes in cold water and drained
½ teaspoon sugar
½ teaspoon light soy sauce
½ teaspoon chicken seasoning powder (or ½ teaspoon fish sauce)
½ teaspoon salt

Heat a wok or skillet and add oil. In batches and on high heat, stir-fry the cabbage, char siu and shrimp. When almost cooked, remove from skillet and set aside. Heat the skillet and stir-fry the bell pepper, two kinds of onions, eggs and bean sprouts. When almost done, remove and set aside. On high heat, add rice noodles, sugar, soy sauce, chicken seasoning powder or fish sauce and salt. Add everything back into the skillet. Mix well and serve.

* The smallest and least expensive shrimp are fine to use in this dish.

火雞粥
Turkey Jook
Turkey Rice Porridge
Feeds a crowd of 20 people

*J*ook, a savory rice porridge, is the ultimate Chinese comfort food. Simple versions are enjoyed by infants and seniors, but even gourmets can savor fancier versions made with raw fish or the delicacy of innards. Variables include type of stock, range of ingredients cooked in the jook and a wide selection of toppings. My mother says the best jook starts with the head and feet of a roasted pig (called siu ji yuk).

20 cups water
1 turkey carcass*
2 pieces chung choy
1 teaspoon white pepper
1 teaspoon salt
½ cup raw peanuts, skinned
1½ cups raw rice, any variety
3 black mushrooms, soaked, stemmed and thinly sliced
1 cup winter melon in ½-inch cubes
½ cup carrots peeled and cut into ¼-inch "coins"
2 cups chopped celery
1 package (6 ounces) dried tofu sticks (foo jook), soaked in cold water overnight
1 cup ground pork or turkey
1 egg
½ teaspoon salt
½ teaspoon pepper
½ can (8 ounces) water chestnuts, chopped
⅛ cup minced green onions
1 cup raw Chinese fish cake

Jook Friday

Alvin Yee suggests the day after Thanksgiving be called Jook Friday instead of Black Friday since many Hawai'i families are using the turkey carcasses to make the delicious rice gruel.

In a large pot, add water, turkey, chung choy, pepper, salt, peanuts and boil for about 1 hour or until water is reduced by half. Remove turkey carcass and chung choy; add rice, mushrooms, winter melon, carrots, celery, and foo jook. Cook for 20 minutes, until rice soup thickens. In a small mixing bowl, combine ground pork or turkey, egg, salt, pepper, water chestnuts and green onions. Form small meatballs and  drop into jook. Add fish cake balls a teaspoon at a time, after dipping spoon in water. Cook 5 minutes more until meatballs and fish cake are cooked. Serve hot with condiments.

Suggested condiments to serve with hot jook include:
Sesame oil
Chopped chung choy, after rinsing
Chopped sweet pickled cucumber (cha gwa)
Chopped green onions
Chopped Chinese parsley
Shredded lettuce
Spicy pickled bamboo shoots
Soy sauce
Chili sauce
Peeled wedges of salt egg (ham dan)
Peeled wedges of preserved 1,000-year-old egg (pei dan)
Slices of raw fish, which will cook when combined with the hot jook

* Substitute ham bone, chicken carcass, roasted pig (siu ji yuk) head or feet.

夏威夷式麵餅
Hawai'i-style Cake Noodle

Makes at least 20 servings, as part of a party buffet

Pan-fried noodles (called Liang Mian Huang) are not uncommon in China, but the fried "cake" is fairly thin and crisp throughout. In Hawai'i we like our cake noodle thick —½ inch to an inch—so while the outside is crisp, the middle is dense and soft. The Chinese version is served as an uncut round; ours is cut into squares or rectangles. Many restaurants claim to have invented this preparation, but it's unclear who really made it famous. However, this must be Hawai'i's favorite Chinese-style noodle and it is a local creation as saimin noodles are usually used to make cake noodles.

12 tablespoons of vegetable oil, divided
1 large clove of garlic, peeled and cut into three pieces
6 packages (9.5 ounces each) saimin noodles*, divided
Large pot of boiling water
1½ teaspoons of salt, divided

Heat a 9- or 10-inch cast iron skillet on high and add 2 tablespoons of oil. Heat one piece of garlic so the oil is flavored. Discard the garlic and keep heat on high. Open the saimin plastic bags and discard the soup packets (or save for another use). Into a large pot of boiling water (and a pasta sieve, if you have one), put in the noodles from 2 packages of noodles. Cook ONLY 2 minutes (instructions will say 3 to 4 minutes), quickly drain the noodles and place in the hot cast iron skillet. Do NOT rinse the noodles. Sprinkle ½ teaspoon of salt over the noodles and press down. Reduce heat to medium-high and cook until noodles are crispy, about 4 minutes. Flip over the "cake" of noodle and add 2 tablespoons of oil around the edge of the skillet. Cook until the second side is brown, about 4 minutes.

Remove from skillet and cool. Cut into 2 x 2-inch squares. Repeat 2 times until all noodles are cooked. Place in a large serving platter and top with vegetables (recipe follows on page 142) and/or Minute Chicken (recipe on page 87).

* In the refrigerated section of grocery stores, or buy about 3½ pounds of saimin noodles from any noodle factory.

(continued on page 142)

Rice and Noodles

Vegetable topping for noodles:

  2 tablespoons vegetable oil
  3 cloves garlic, minced
  1 tablespoon minced ginger
  ½ onion, sliced top to root
  6 large heads baby bok choy (also
      called Shanghai cabbage),
      chopped into 1-inch pieces
  12 tablespoons vegetable oil,
      divided
  ¼ cup oyster sauce
  ½ cup chicken broth
  ½ teaspoon ground pepper
  2 tablespoons cornstarch mixed in
      4 tablespoons cold water or chicken broth

**Garnishes: ¼ cup chopped green onions
    and ¼ cup chopped Chinese parsley**

In the same skillet, add oil and stir-fry the garlic, ginger and onion for about 3 minutes on high. Add bok choy, oyster sauce, broth and pepper and cook until bok choy is wilted. Add cornstarch mixture and cook until thickened, about 2 minutes on high. Pour over cake noodles. If you aren't serving it immediately, keep the cake noodles separate from the topping (pui tau) until just before serving or let people serve themselves the gravy. Garnish with green onions and Chinese parsley.

Birthday Noodles

Noodles are considered a symbol of long life and birthday celebrations must include them. In Hawai'i, thick squares of cake noodle are sometimes served at birthday dinners, but alas, the cut noodle is a bad omen for longevity as the noodle is not continuous. Many people forget the symbolism.

Chicago Noodles

Many people I talked to wistfully remember the delicious texture and taste of what they called Chicago noodles. What they recall is a five-pound box of dried noodles sold by a Chicago factory through the 1980s. No one could remember the actual brand, just the name Chicago.

炒麵
Chow Mein
Fried Noodles
Makes 8 servings

Florence Chew Gum Wong Lee was more of a baker than a cook, but she did make noodles. As children, we used to make fun of our grandmother's Chinese name, Chew Gum, which means gold.

1 box (16 ounces) dried wheat noodles
1 tablespoon salt
1 tablespoon vegetable oil
3 cups vegetable oil
½ pound string beans or broccoli
3 stalks celery, cut thinly on the diagonal
2 carrots, julienned
2 onions, cut in slivers with the grain (from stem to root)
3 stalks green onion, cut into 1-inch pieces
2 cloves garlic, minced
1 finger-sized piece of ginger, minced
1 can (12 ounces) Spam® or 1 cup shredded chicken
2 cans (14.5 ounces each) chicken broth or 1¾ cups freshly made
   chicken broth
3 tablespoons cornstarch dissolved in 4 tablespoons of the broth
2 tablespoons sugar
1 teaspoon five-spice powder
2 tablespoons soy sauce
Garnishes: chopped green onions and Chinese parsley
Condiments: Chinese red vinegar or Chinese mustard and soy sauce

Boil 3 quarts of water and add salt. Cook noodles for 5 minutes. Drain and add vegetable oil to noodles to separate noodles. In a deep skillet, add oil and deep-fry noodles until crispy, brown, and look like a pancake.

Set aside noodles on a serving platter with rim. In the skillet, stir-fry string beans, celery, carrots, onions, green onions, garlic, ginger, and meat. Make gravy using broth, cornstarch mixture, sugar, Chinese five-spice powder, and soy sauce; cook over medium heat until thickened. Add in sautéed vegetables and meat and pour over noodles to cover. Garnish with green onions and Chinese parsley. Serve immediately with Chinese red vinegar or Chinese mustard with soy sauce.

冬菇韭黃伊麵

E-Mein with Mushrooms and Yellow Chives

Makes 4 servings

In Hong Kong, wheat noodles that are fried, then dried (called e-mein, e-foo mein or yee foo mein), are served at birthday parties as a symbol of long life. Traditionally made with black mushrooms and yellow garlic chives, the flavor of the toppings (called pui tow) is mild. The focus is on the chewy and soft texture of the noodles. Some restaurants add crab meat or lobster to make the dish more luxurious. You cook the dried noodles in water to soften it to the desired texture.*

1 "cake" E-mein, 9 inches in diameter and 2 inches high
6 dried black mushrooms, soaked in ½ cup hot water, stems removed, and thinly sliced (reserve liquid)
½ cup fresh abalone mushrooms cut into ¼-inch wide matchsticks*
½ cup sliced fresh white mushrooms
¼ cup oyster or abalone sauce
1 cup yellow chives cut into 1-inch lengths**
1 teaspoon sesame oil
Garnishes: chopped green onions and Chinese parsley

Boil a pot of water. Cook noodles until the desired texture, about 5 minutes. Drain. In a separate pot, simmer the mushrooms in the black mushroom liquid and the oyster sauce until tender, about 5 minutes. Add chives and cook 2 more minutes. Add sesame oil and pour sauce over noodles. Toss and serve immediately.

* Also called ali'i mushrooms, king, oyster, and eryngi mushrooms. To showcase these expensive mushrooms, cut in slices, stir-fry until cooked for garnish.
** Yellow chives are Chinese garlic chives (gau choy) which are covered to keep them from getting green from sunlight.

水餃湯
Easy Homemade Dumplings in Soup
Makes about 8 servings

Mung Mung (pull apart) Mein is a fun dish to make with children because the dumplings don't have to be perfect to be delicious. Other families may have different names for this dish, but we called it Mung Mung Dumplings. I have fond and fun memories of making this at my cousin Pam Ching Leong's home with her daughters, Lee-Anne, JoAnne and Erin, when we were young. There was flour everywhere! Some people roll out the dough and cut it into noodles, but we made freestyle dumplings. Pam says whatever shape you make is fine, this is a commoner's soul food!

Soup:
- 1 tablespoon vegetable oil
- 1 pound ground pork
- 3 tablespoons shrimp paste (ham ha)
- 2 chung choy, minced
- 6 cups chicken broth
- 6 cups water
- Salt to taste
- 4 cups all-purpose flour, plus extra, if necessary
- 1 egg

Garnishes: chopped green onions, Chinese parsley, sesame oil and sliced char siu (optional)

In a large stockpot over high heat, add oil and brown pork. Add shrimp paste, chung choy, chicken broth, and water. Bring to a boil, then lower heat to medium and simmer for 30 minutes. Add salt to taste.

In a large mixing bowl, mix the flour and egg with enough water (about 4 cups) so it can be handled. Knead the dough for at least 5 minutes. Use your hands to pull dough to make a small ball and press it flat on a lightly floured surface to form 2-inch pancakes. Coat dough with flour and put aside. When all the pancakes are done, add them to the soup broth and cook until tender, about 20 to 30 minutes (it depends how thick you make your pancakes). On a slow boil, the broth will get thicker and thicker.

Serve hot and garnish with chopped green onions, Chinese parsley, sesame oil, and char siu or no garnish at all.

星洲炒米
Singapore Rice Noodles
Makes 4 to 6 servings

This curry-flavored dish is one of the most popular noodle dishes worldwide. It's not so strange that the Chinese repertoire includes curry, given the centuries that India and China have traded goods. Several other Chinese dishes also use curry as a flavoring, among them curry beef tomato and curried long rice with crab.

12 ounces rice-stick noodles (mai fun)
3 tablespoons vegetable oil, divided
2 slices bacon, cut into matchsticks
2 tablespoons dried shrimp (ha mai), soaked in water, then minced
1 large onion (about 1 cup), sliced
½ green bell pepper, cored and cut into matchsticks
2 eggs, beaten
¼ pound Chinese barbecue pork (char siu), sliced into matchsticks
½ teaspoon salt
2½ tablespoons curry powder*
5 tablespoons chicken broth
1½ tablespoons light soy sauce
½ pound shrimp, peeled, deveined and cut in half lengthwise
2 cups bean sprouts
2 stalks green onions, cut in 1-inch diagonal slices

Soak the dried noodles in hot water for at least 20 minutes until tender. Drain well and set aside.

In a wok or skillet, add 1 tablespoon of oil on high heat. When hot, add bacon, dried shrimp, onions and green peppers; cook for about 2 minutes. Remove from heat and set aside. Add 1 tablespoon of oil on high heat and cook eggs for 2 minutes. When stirring, cut into pieces. Place on bacon, shrimp, onion and pepper mixture. Add last tablespoon of oil and heat wok. Add in noodles, char siu, salt, curry, chicken broth and soy sauce with the raw shrimp and cook for 2 minutes. Add in the mixture that was set aside with bean sprouts and green onions and cook for 2 more minutes. Serve hot.

* Adjust the amount of curry depending on personal taste.

叉燒炒粉
Char Siu Chow Funn
Stir-Fried Rice Noodles with Char Siu and Vegetables

From Keoni Chang, corporate chef at Foodland

Makes 6 servings

In Hawai'i, we love all forms of noodles whether they are spelled funn or fun. Look funn is made from rice flour and steamed. When we stir-fry (called chow) the noodles, they become Chow Funn. Most of us buy our noodles from the grocery store or noodle factory, but some people do make them at home. Chef Keoni talks about frying the noodles at a high enough heat and for enough time so the edges are browned or slightly charred. There are many varieties of toppings for the chow funn, but this is a popular version. I like to serve it with a dipping sauce of Chinese red vinegar or a mixture of Chinese hot mustard and soy sauce.

3 tablespoons vegetable oil, divided
½ pound Chinese barbecue pork (char siu) or roast pork, thinly sliced
½ pound ham, thinly sliced
1 thumb-sized piece ginger, minced
½ cup thinly slivered carrots
½ cup thinly sliced celery
¼ cup sliced onions
2 cups bean sprouts
2 tablespoons oyster sauce
1 package (12 ounces) cooked and refrigerated rice noodles (called look funn before cooking and chow funn after cooking)
2 stalks green onions, cut in 1-inch lengths
Garnishes: slivered green onions, char siu, and carrots

Heat one tablespoon of oil in a skillet or wok. Stir-fry the meat with ginger until lightly browned. Add carrots, celery and onions and cook until half done. Add bean sprouts and stir lightly. Remove everything from the pan. Heat pan and add remaining vegetable oil. Rinse chow funn in water to separate the noodles. Drain and add chow fun and cook 1 minute or until the desired level of browning on edges of noodle is achieved. Toss in the meat and vegetable mixture. Taste and add more oyster sauce or soy sauce, if desired. Garnish with green onions just before serving and add additional slivers of char siu and carrots, if desired.

素菜
Vegetables

Chinese take their vegetables seriously. Unlike traditional Western culinary culture, vegetables are not an afterthought, they are a main consideration.

Many of Hawai'i's plantation workers were from humble roots and couldn't afford much meat. In southern China, a complete meal would be rice, some vegetables, perhaps flavored with bits of protein such as slivers of pork or flakes of salted fish (ham yu). More common would be vegetables with fermented soy bean (dau foo mui) or salted black soy beans (dau see).

Vegetables were widely available as they could be grown in home gardens, but rarely were eaten raw. Instead, the Chinese like their vegetables in soups, stir-fried, salted, dried, pickled, steamed, braised, simmered, and boiled. Although the methods vary greatly, there is a traditional way for most individual vegetables that varies by region.

Ask how to cook bitter melon and a Cantonese will immediately suggest stir-frying with garlic or thinly sliced beef, or stuffing the round melon with a ground pork mixture and simmering or steaming, sometimes including salted black beans. Other regions will add bitter melon to soup or pickle it.

Thinner, more watery vegetables, such as swamp cabbage (kang kong or ong choy), spinach, Chinese spinach or watercress are usually showcased in soups or stir-fried quickly so their shape is maintained.

Firmer, more dense vegetables—carrots, broccoli, Chinese broccoli (gai lan), and cauliflower—are sliced in uniform shapes and stir-fried with a sauce or protein.

Except for pickles, all vegetables are served very hot, as if they have just come off the wok.

腐乳炒西洋菜
Watercress with Fermented Tofu Sauce

Makes 4 servings

Fermented white bean curd is an acquired taste, but it could become your favorite seasoning when preparing leafy vegetables. The technique used here is also a good way to cook "watery vegetables" such as spinach, ong choy, romaine, or Mānoa and butter lettuce. On menus in Zhongshan, China, dishes with this flavoring are titled "Homestyle Cooking." The fermented tofu comes in 1-inch cubes and is sold in bottles with liquid.

> 1 large bunch watercress, about 9 cups
> 2 tablespoons vegetable oil
> 4 cloves garlic, minced
> ½ teaspoon salt
> ½ teaspoon sugar
> ¼ teaspoon ground white pepper
> 2 squares of fermented white bean curd (dou foo mui or foo yu)
> 3 tablespoons water, if needed

Cut watercress into 1 to 1½-inch lengths. Discard the bottom 1 to 2 inches if tough. Soak in water to remove any dirt; drain.

Heat a wok or skillet and add oil. When oil is hot, add garlic and stir in watercress. There will be some remaining water on the watercress. There's no need to dry the watercress. Stir frequently on high heat until watercress is wilted and tender, about 5 minutes. Add salt, sugar, peper, and fermented bean cubes. Simmer 5 minutes more. Add water, if needed. Serve hot.

Don't Trust the Dishwasher?

At many Zhongshan restaurants, pots of hot water and a bowl are brought to your table. Customers wash all silverware, including chopsticks, and all plates and bowls. Some feel that too much of the restaurant's harsh cleaning liquid remains on the dishes; others that not enough cleanser was used.

蝦醬通菜
Ham Ha Ong Choy
Chinese Water Spinach
with Preserved Shrimp Sauce
Makes 6 servings

Ham ha is a delicious secret weapon with a bold umami flavor. A bit of sugar tempers the strong flavor and makes the dish outstanding. Ong choy goes by many names—water spinach, water morning glory, kangkong, swamp cabbage. If you can't find it, spinach is a nice substitute. In Hong Kong I was served half a head of young romaine lettuce cooked with ham ha in a clay pot. It was very good and the lettuce remained crisp.

1 bunch raw ong choy, about 4 cups
1 tablespoon vegetable oil
1 tablespoon fermented shrimp paste (ham ha)
2 cloves garlic, smashed
1 teaspoon sugar

Cut the hard ends off the ong choy and discard. Cut remainder into 1½-inch pieces. Soak in water to remove dirt; drain. In a wok or sauce pan, heat oil on high heat. Add ham ha and garlic and stir. Because the stems take longer to cook than the leaves, add stems in first with sugar. About 5 minutes later, add the leaves. Cook until wilted, about 10 minutes. Serve hot.

乾炒豆角
Quick-Fried String Beans

From Good Chinese Cooking by Grace W. Kwok
Makes 4 servings as part of a multi-course meal

Dr. Daniel Kwok, well-known China historian at the University of Hawai'i, edited his mother's cookbook. He creatively substituted fish sauce whenever an old recipe called for monosodium glutamate (MSG). Just brilliant. This is a classic side dish.

1 pound string beans, remove ends and fibers
2 tablespoons oil
½ teaspoon salt
2 tablespoons light soy sauce
1 tablespoon sherry
1 teaspoon fish sauce
½ teaspoon sugar

Wash and cut string beans into 1½-inch sections. Heat oil in a hot skillet. Add beans and stir for 1 minute. Add the remaining ingredients, stir, cover and reduce to low heat. Cook for 2 to 3 minutes until beans are the consistency you desire. Serve on platter as a side dish.

Simple, Fresh

I was reminded of the value of keeping things simple in Zhongshan where one restaurant served one of the most common vegetables, Napa cabbage, or won bok, sliced lengthwise and simmered in a plain chicken, pork or seafood broth until sweet. Delicious and so simple—just accentuating the naturalness of the vegetable.

客家鹹菜
Hakka Ham Choy
Chinese Salted Vegetables Hakka Style

Moilee Ho Hong taught me this Hakka version of preserved vegetables, called ham choy, or salted vegetable.

Wash mustard cabbage, head cabbage or turnip. Cut into bite-sized pieces and put into a glass or ceramic bowl or jar.

Wash rice and pour the water over the vegetables; add rock salt and cover with a plate weighed down by something heavy. Leave at room temperature for one week.

Mrs. Hong says you will know when the vegetables are ready because you will smell the fermentation, a process started by the rice water. Because it is not a sweet type of preservation, you'll want to add sugar when you cook the vegetables.

The fermented vegetables can be sautéed with sliced pork belly, with Chinese slab sugar added. This is a true Hakka dish! Mrs. Hong was born in 1912 and still cooks when she has a craving.

1941 - 43   Tan Lo

羅梓騰

My grandfather, Tan Lo, was president of Tsung Tsin Association, the organization for Hakkas in Hawai'i.

酸菜
Tsin Choy
Pickled Mustard Cabbage

From Esther "Dede" Lo Chinn

Makes about 5 pint jars

For tsin choy, I prefer the crunch from the bottoms of the mustard cabbage stalks over the leaves. Sometimes in Chinatown you can buy mustard cabbage with the leaves already cut off. Otherwise, save the leafy parts for a good soup.

5 pounds fresh mustard cabbage
½ cup rock salt
4 cups sugar
3 cups white vinegar

Clean each leaf, paying close attention to the bottoms as they tend to capture dirt.* Cut cabbage into 1-inch pieces. Wash and drain. Mix with salt and let sit unrefrigerated for at least 1 hour. Drain water, but do not rinse off salt. Boil sugar and vinegar until sugar is dissolved. Cool. Stuff clean jars with salted, wilted cabbage. Fill with the sugar/vinegar mixture. Cover and leave unrefrigerated for one day. Then refrigerate and eat plain or stir-fry with squid or pork (see recipe on page 157).

* An easy way to clean the cut cabbage is to drop it in a big bowl of water and toss the cabbage in the water. Then gently scoop out the cabbage and drain excess water. You'll see the dirt sinking to the bottom of the bowl.

Variation: Use the same method to pickle bitter melon, seeded and sliced lengthwise in diagonal pieces less than ¼-inch wide. I first had bitter melon prepared this way at a Shanghai restaurant discovered by my friend Cassandra Pan. The dish was so refreshing, and only a bit of the bitterness remained.

酸菜魷魚
Tsin Choy with Squid

Makes 4 servings as part of a multi-course meal

Pickled mustard cabbage (called tsin choy) with squid is a classic home-style dish that is very common in Hawai'i. Every family's tsin choy is different—one might be more sweet and another more vinegary. You'll need to adjust the recipe to the kind of tsin choy you have. This is made with the Tsin Choy recipe on page 155.

- 1 tablespoon vegetable or peanut oil
- 1 large clove garlic, smashed
- 2-inch piece ginger, peeled and sliced
- 2 cups pickled mustard cabbage (tsin choy, see recipe on page 155), drained, liquid reserved
- ½ tablespoon light soy sauce
- 3 tablespoons sugar
- 2 tablespoons cider vinegar
- 1½ tablespoons cornstarch mixed in 3 tablespoons cold water
- 1 pound squid, cleaned and cut into tentacles and 1-inch rings (results in about 2 cups of cleaned, cut squid)

In a skillet, heat the oil and stir-fry the garlic and ginger for 3 minutes. Cut the tsin choy into smaller pieces if they are too large. Stir in tsin choy with liquid, soy sauce, sugar and vinegar for 10 minutes. Tsin choy should still be a bit crunchy. Add in cornstarch mixture and cook for 3 minutes. Taste and add additional cider vinegar or sugar after tasting. Add in squid during last few minutes and cook until tender, about 1 minute. Do not overcook the squid.

Variation: Instead of squid, clean and slice ½ pound of pork. Marinate it in the soy sauce. Follow the recipe above, but add the pork and cook until tender, about 20 minutes.

蝦米炒黃瓜
Cucumbers and Dried Shrimp

From Lorna Lo

Makes 6 servings

This was one of the most common dishes my mother would make for dinner. It wasn't a main course, just an easy vegetable side that we enjoyed. She probably made it so often because cucumbers were inexpensive and she always had dried shrimp in the pantry. Somehow the sweetness of the cooked cucumbers pairs with the saltiness of the shrimp to create a magical dish.

20 dried shrimp (ha mai), about 1 ounce
1 pound cucumbers (about 3)
2 tablespoons cooking oil
¼ teaspoon black pepper
Garnish: green onions cut in 1-inch length (optional)

Soak shrimp in ½ cup of hot water for at least 30 minutes. Reserve water. Clean any remaining shells or veins. Keep shrimp whole or chop. If you buy the most common everyday cucumbers, peel and cut them lengthwise and seed them. Then cut the cucumbers into ½-inch slices. If you buy the smaller, but longer Japanese cucumbers, you do not need to peel or seed them, just cut them into ½-inch slices. Heat oil in a skillet and sauté the shrimp for two minutes. Add cucumbers, the reserved water from the shrimp and pepper; cook on medium heat for 10 to 15 minutes, until cucumbers are translucent. Add additional water if needed. Add green onions and cook two minutes more. Garnish and serve hot or at room temperature.

Dried Shrimp—Ha Mai

This flavor enhancer comes in all sizes and grades of quality. With lower grades, pieces of shell need to be removed and the black entrails cleaned off. But just a small amount of this savory addition makes a huge difference. My friend, Roger Yu, said that adding reconstituted minced dried shrimp into his fried rice, as suggested in an old Gail Wong cookbook, "revolutionized" his dish. The smallest size of shrimp is good in No Mai Fan, Chinese Sticky Rice (page 132), as it doesn't need to be chopped at all.

芋頭炆燒肉
Taro with Roast Pork

From Sylvianne Yee

Makes 4 servings

Sylvianne prefers Hawaiian taro for this dish because it gets more gooey than Chinese taro. In this case, gooey is good.

2 taro corms (about 4 pounds), washed peeled and cut into thin wedges
1 tablespoon oil
1-inch piece ginger, minced
2 cloves garlic, minced
1 pound roast pork (siu ji yuk), cut into 1-inch pieces
2 teaspoons fermented shrimp paste (ham ha)
1 teaspoon salt
1 teaspoon sugar
Water to cover ingredients
Chopped green onions for garnish

In a large sauce pan, heat oil and fry taro pieces with ginger and garlic for 5 minutes. Add roast pork with fermented shrimp paste, salt, sugar and fry about 5 minutes more. Add water to barely cover ingredients. Cover and reduce heat to low and simmer for 3 hours, stirring occasionally.

When taro is soft and a bit mushy, the dish is done. Sprinkle with green onions for garnish.

臘腸豆角
Long Beans with Chinese Sausage
Makes 4 to 6 servings

long beans have always been a favorite of our family. They're easy to prepare and the texture and taste of the beans are so enjoyable.

4 lup cheong sausages, cut diagonally
1½ tablespoons vegetable oil
6 cloves garlic, smashed
1-inch piece ginger, peeled and sliced
1 pound long beans (dau gok), discard hard end, cut in 1½-inch pieces
½ cup water
2 teaspoons oyster sauce
1 teaspoon chili sauce or sriracha (optional)

In a small pot, cover sausages with water. Bring to a boil and cook 2 minutes. Drain sausages on a plate lined with paper towels. In a wok or skillet, heat the oil on high and add garlic and ginger; stir constantly for 2 minutes. Add sausage and stir-fry for 2 minutes. Rinse beans in a colander, drain and add to skillet. Cook for 2 minutes. Add water and oyster sauce; cook for 10 minutes or until beans are tender, yet still crunchy. Cook longer if you prefer beans with a softer texture. Add chili sauce or sriracha sauce, if desired, and serve immediately.

Substitution:
Instead of the usual sweet Chinese sausage, try liver lup cheong, the soul food variation.

羅漢齋
Lo Han Jai
New Year's Monks Food
Serves a crowd of 25 or more

At the start of each lunar new year, it is mandatory to eat the traditional vegetarian stew called Lo Han (the lower gods) Jai. Each family makes it slightly differently, some more saucy, some with more fermented bean curd, and some sweeter. This version is based on the recipe served by my maternal grandfather, John Sau Lee. Sometimes he would include expensive dried oysters, which I thought was wrong as the dish should be vegetarian, until I learned that the word for the oysters is hau see, which means "good things." Chinese like to invite good luck with words that sound like good tidings.

Sauce:
- 3 tablespoons vegetable or peanut oil
- 9 cubes red fermented bean curd (nam yue)
- 18 cubes white fermented bean curd (dau foo mui) and ½ cup of the liquid from the bottle
- 4-inch piece fresh ginger, peeled, sliced and pounded

- 2 sticks Chinese slab sugar (wong tong) or ¾ cup packed brown sugar (bing tong)
- 2 dried star anise (ba gok)
- 2 tablespoons rock salt
- ¼ cup sherry or whiskey (jow)
- 3 tablespoons hoisin sauce
- 6 cups water

Dried ingredients (Soak in water the day before cooking):
- 2 packages (14 ounces each) dried bean curd sticks (foo jook)
- ¼ cup dried lotus seeds (lyan jee)
- 6 large dried black mushrooms (doong goo), stems cut off and quartered
- 4 ounces dried lily flower, also called tiger lily buds, but actually the dried flower of the orange day lily (gum choy), hard tips cut off
- 6 red dates or jujubes (hung jo)

Large fistful of dried hair
   seaweed (fat choy)
1½ packages (7.75 ounce) long
   rice (Nice brand preferred)
1 cup cloud ear fungus (chin
   ngee)
Dried chestnuts, dried
   bamboo shoots and peanuts
   (optional)

Canned ingredients:
2 cans (15 ounces each) bamboo shoot tips, drain, rinse and cut into
   1-inch slices
2 cans (8 ounces each) button mushrooms, drain and rinse
2 cans (15 ounces each) baby corn, drain, rinse and cut in half at a
   slight diagonal
2 cans (14 ounces each) gingko nuts (can substitute garbanzo beans)
   drain and rinse
1 can (8 ounces) sliced water
   chestnuts, drain and rinse

Other ingredients:
½ pound snow peas, tough
   ends pinched off
4 packages (3 ounces each)
   fried tofu (dau foo pei) or
   aburage in Japanese, cut
   into ½-inch strips
1 pound fresh lotus root, peeled and sliced into ¼-inch rounds, then
   quartered
3 carrots, peeled and sliced diagonally
1 large head Napa cabbage (won bok), sliced into 1-inch pieces
3 tablespoons sesame seeds

   Cut softened foo jook into 4-inch pieces. Boil in water for about 10
minutes or until tender. Blanch snow peas. Blanch fried tofu in water to
remove excess oil. Set aside.

   In a large pot (you may want to split this into two pots) boil all the
sauce ingredients for 5 minutes. Add in lotus seeds, lotus root, black
mushrooms, lily flowers, bamboo shoots and red dates and simmer 20

(continued on the next page)

minutes. Add in carrots, foo jook, seaweed, long rice, fried tofu, cloud ear fungus, canned mushrooms, baby corn, gingko nuts, and water chestnuts. Simmer 20 more minutes. Add won bok and cook for 10 more minutes. Add more water if needed. Test for doneness. When tender, garnish with snow peas and sesame seeds. Serve hot or at room temperature with lettuce and extra dau foo mui.

Easy Jai

Include just long rice and the canned ingredients. Cook in sauce with only half the water.

Budget Jai

Omit the most expensive vegetables: seaweed, dried mushrooms, lotus seeds and root, lily flower, and cloud ear fungus.

High End Jai

Omit canned mushrooms and baby corn. Use fresh foo jook, bamboo shoots, gingkos, water chestnuts, and shiitake mushrooms.

Auspicious Foods

Chinese are superstitious and there is symbolism in this dish.

- **Gingko nuts** look like gold or silver ingots
- **Hair seaweed** is called Fat Choy like the greeting "Gung Hee Fat Choy"
- **Long rice noodles** represent longevity
- **Lily buds (gum choy)** are gold, which symbolizes wealth
- **Lotus root and lotus seeds** promise or endurance (from the mud grows the beautiful and useful plant)
- **Napa cabbage (won bok)** represents wealth (pai tsai in Mandarin)
- **Oysters (hau see),** also means good things or good fortune
- **Red date** because red is a good luck color in the Chinese culture
- **Sesame seeds** for children/ fertility
- **Lettuce** represents wealth and riches Sheng Tsai (Mandarin)
- And we American children would pronounce **Napa cabbage (won bok)** "One Buck," meaning money!

臺式醃黃瓜
Taiwan-style Pickled Cucumber

From Linda Chang Wyrgatsch

Makes about a quart

Τhe easy 1-1-1 pickling sauce used to make these delicious and refreshing crunchy pickles can also be used with ginger or turnips. You'll want to make this over and over.

1 cup soy sauce
1 cup sugar
1 cup white or apple cider vinegar
6 cucumbers, washed, ends removed, cut into 2-inch long halves*
2 to 4 Hawaiian chili peppers, smashed (optional)

In a pot, combine soy sauce, sugar and vinegar; cook over medium heat until sugar is dissolved. Cool. Put cucumbers in a glass or plastic container. Pour pickling mixture over. Keep unrefrigerated for 1 day, then store in the refrigerator. Eat after one day; will keep for several weeks.

* You can cut the cucumbers in any shape you like. If you have more pickling liquid, add more cucumbers. Some like a spicier pickle, so add Hawaiian chili peppers.

No Cold Water

Hawai'i popos (grandmothers) and goong goongs (grandfathers) used to say, "Don't ever drink cold water. It's bad for your digestion." Even today in a Chinese restaurant, when you ask for water, chances are you will be asked "hot or cold?" In China I was served hot or room-temperature water when I asked for something to drink.

甜点
Sweets

The Chinese are not known for their desserts. When we were growing up, it was more common for simple whole fruits to end a meal. Oranges and tangerines symbolize strength and perseverance. Mangoes, lychee, and longan were always enjoyed, as were mountain apples, and all melons. Even apples, pears, and bananas were savored.

When we do have dessert it is often Almond Tofu, also called Almond Float when it was served with mandarin oranges, fruit cocktail, or canned lychee. More Western-style cookies with almond flavoring or sesame seeds are also popular.

For Hawai'i's Chinese, a common dessert is dau lau. Made from sticky rice (no mai) flour and water, the dough is rolled into dumplings and boiled until tender, then rolled in toasted sesame seeds, shredded coconut, ground peanuts, and sugar.

芝麻餅
Sesame Cookies

From Ava Wong
Makes about 4 dozen

his recipe was given to Patricia Linda Lau at her wedding shower in 1968 and is still a family favorite. The cookies will bake up pale; for a darker look, toast the sesame seeds in a pan for about five minutes over low to medium heat. Careful—they burn easily.

2 cups flour
¼ teaspoon salt
½ cup butter
¼ cup shortening
1 cup sugar
1 egg
1 teaspoon vanilla
½ cup sesame seeds

Preheat oven to 375°F. Sift together flour and salt. Set aside. Cream together butter, shortening, and sugar. Add egg and vanilla and mix in the flour and salt. Shape into walnut-sized balls and dip one side of ball into the sesame seeds. Place sesame seed side up on an ungreased or parchment paper lined baking sheet. Gently press cookies to make the dough level. Bake for 12 to 15 minutes. Cool and serve.

芝麻薄餅
Paper Thin Sesame Seed Cookies
From Mabel Wang
Makes 6 to 7 dozen cookies

My grandaunt, Mabel Wang, was a wonderful cook and volunteer. After my granduncle, Yan Chin "Ted" Wang, retired from the Queen's Medical Center's radiology department, they spent years in Zaire, Zimbabwe, and Taiwan, volunteering to establish radiology centers in cities that had no such services. Uncle Ted changed the spelling of his last name, Wong, to the Mandarin way to match the spelling on his diplomas. This cookie of Aunt Mabel's isn't a traditional Chinese treat, but is very buttery and delicious.

1 cup butter, at room temperature
1 cup sugar
1 egg, at room temperature
1 teaspoon vanilla
2 cups flour
½ teaspoon baking soda
¼ teaspoon salt (½ teaspoon if kosher salt)
1 cup toasted sesame seeds, divided

Cream butter and sugar together. Add egg and vanilla and mix well. Sift flour with baking soda and salt. Add in butter mixture. Add ¾ cup of the sesame seeds. Mix. Place mounds (a scant teaspoon) of dough on a cookie sheet lined with parchment paper and flatten with a metal spoon dipped in ice water, until paper-thin. Top with a sprinkling of sesame seeds.*

In a 350°F oven, bake 12 to 15 minutes or until golden brown. Slide parchment paper off hot cookie sheet to cool immediately. When these cookies cool, they become brittle and will break easily.

* The sesame seed topping wasn't in Auntie Mabel's original recipe, but I think it adds to the attractiveness of the cookie.

杏仁餅
Flaky Almond Cookies

Makes about 24 small cookies

This recipe makes delicate, delicious cookies.

1 cup flour
½ teaspoon baking powder
½ teaspoon kosher salt
½ cup vegetable shortening
½ cup sugar
1 teaspoon almond extract
1 egg yolk
1 teaspoon water
24 blanched whole almonds

Sift flour, baking powder and salt together in a small bowl. In a bowl or mixer, combine shortening, sugar and almond extract; mix until fluffy. Add flour mixture in three batches. Make sure it is thoroughly mixed.

On parchment or waxed paper, roll mixture into quarter-sized roll and refrigerate for 1 hour.

Preheat oven to 350°F. Cut the cookie dough into 24 pieces. Round the edges and put on a baking tray lined with parchment or silpat. Mix the egg yolk with 1 tablespoon of water. Brush the egg mixture on the cookies. Press each cookie with a whole almond.

Bake for 20 minutes. At 10 minutes, rotate the cookie sheet. Cool and serve.

Lychee in Hawai'i

The first lychee tree brought from China to Hawai'i was planted at the home of Chun Afong, at the corner of Nu'uanu Avenue and School Street. The home was sold to the Chun Hoon family who then built Chun Hoon Market at that location.

杏仁豆腐
Almond Gelatin Dessert

From Marsha Chan Gishi, through her brother Wesley Chan
Makes 20 (4-ounce) servings

he agar agar makes this recipe very fragile and this dessert will break apart easily, especially if poured in a pan or bowl that is too deep.

2 sticks agar agar gelatin (.07 ounce or 20 grams for 2 sticks)
3 cups cold water
1¾ cups sugar
6 cups (1% fat) milk
4½ teaspoons almond extract
Canned fruits (optional)

Tear agar agar and soak in water for 30 minutes in sauce pan. Cook over medium heat, stirring frequently, until agar agar is completely dissolved (if there are undissolved particles, the agar agar solution may need to be strained).

Add sugar and cook, uncovered, for 15 minutes stirring frequently. Stir in milk and remove from heat. Add almond extract and allow to cool.

Pour into shallow 9 x 13 inch pan, filling to 1½ to 2 inches deep and refrigerate overnight. To serve, cut into cubes or desired sizes and serve with canned fruit cocktail, mandarin oranges or lychee, with or without the sweetened juices from the can.

*"French eat enthusiastically,
the English eat apologetically."*

—CHINESE WRITER LIN YUTANG

"And the Chinese eat continuously,"

ADDS DR. DANIEL KWOK, RETIRED UNIVERSITY OF
HAWAI'I PROFESSOR OF CHINESE HISTORY

年糕
Nien Gao
New Year's Gao

Adapted by Linda Lo Young from her mother Rosie Chock Lo,
who learned it from her mother Moi Lum Chock
3 batches make 4 large gao formed in glass bowls
(8½ inches in diameter and 2½ inches deep)

During the new year celebration, eating the sticky rice pudding (called gao) is a must. Sesame seeds symbolize children and the red from the red dates is always good luck in the Chinese culture. The stickiness of the dessert symbolizes the family staying together. This is one of the best tasting and softest texture gaos. Make 3 batches so you can use a mixer.

1½ cups water
1 pound Chinese slab sugar
   (wong tong; dark sugar can
   be substituted, but it will be
   different)
½ cup dark brown sugar
2 pieces of canned yams (each
   the size of a finger)
1 pound sweet rice flour
¼ cup vegetable oil
1 can (14 ounces) coconut milk
½ cup freshly grated coconut
   (fresh is best, but you can use
   frozen)
Vegetable oil spray
Foil
4 Chinese red dates
   (1 for each bowl)
About 3 tablespoons toasted
   sesame seeds
2 double steamers or 4 single
   steamers*

Gao with Egg

Our family would rarely have any leftover gao, but after a few days, if it became hard, the elders would pan fry it with or without oil so it turned soft in the inside with a great crust on the outside. Another favorite way was to dip the hardened gao in a beaten egg and fry it so it would have an egg covering.

Dissolve the two sugars in hot water, then cool. With an electric mixer, blend yams. Mix in the sugar mixture. Then gradually add in flour, oil, coconut milk and coconut. Mix until there is no trace of the yams. Lightly spray the inside of the glass bowls with vegetable oil spray. Make two more batches. Pour mixture into the glass bowls and equalize the 4 bowls. Cover with foil. Put in a steamer for 5 hours. After 3 hours, you may want to rotate the top steamer with the lower one. Refill water as needed. The longer you steam it, the darker and more caramel tasting this dessert will become.

Remove from steamer, immediately remove foil and spray the top with vegetable oil to seal it. Sprinkle the top with sesame seeds and place a red date in the center. Let cool overnight. In the morning, turn out into a plate. It's easiest cut with a plastic knife.

* Linda recommends stacking no more than two layers in a steamer.

Variation: Clean 24 ti leaves and remove the hard middle core. Line each bowl with 6 ti leaves before steaming. Some people enjoy the flavor from the ti leaves.

豆撈

Dau Lau

Chinese Sweet Rice Balls in Peanut, Coconut, Sesame Coating

Makes about 40 balls

This easy dessert may be served any time of the year, but it is especially popular during New Year festivities as a substitute for the New Year's steamed rice pudding (called nien gao). Like gao, Dau Lau, a sticky treat, symbolizes family unity. Its coatings are also auspicious: peanuts for longevity, coconut for close relationships, and sesame seeds as a symbol of children or fertility. The treat is so simple that even young children can help prepare the balls before boiling or roll them in the peanut coating before serving.

Rice balls:
   1 pound sweet rice (no mai) flour
   2 cups water

Coating:
   1½ cups roasted peanuts, chopped
   ¼ cup toasted sesame seeds
   ⅔ cup sugar
   1 cup grated or shredded unsweetened coconut

In a bowl, mix flour with water to make a stiff dough. Roll into 1-inch balls. This makes about 40 balls. In a large pot, bring at least 10 cups water to a boil and put 8 to 10 balls into the water at a time. When the balls float to the top (about 2 to 3 minutes), cook them for 2 more minutes. Drain and repeat in batches until all the balls are cooked.

Roll balls in peanut, sesame, sugar, and coconut mixture until thoroughly coated and serve immediately.

Variation: Finely chop ¼ cup preserved sweetened winter melon. Before cooking, flatten the rice ball and make a pocket; add pieces of melon in the center of dough, gather edges around filling, pinch to seal and roll into a ball. Add balls into the boiling water and cook as directed above.

芝麻糊

Black Sesame Pudding

From Pauline Chu who learned it from her mother Cheng Yuk King
Makes 10 to 12 servings

This dessert is commonly served throughout China and Taiwan.

1 cup short-grain white rice, washed and soaked in 1 cup water and refrigerated overnight
2 cups black sesame seeds, soaked in 2 cups water and refrigerated overnight
8 cups water
2 cups brown sugar, packed

Using a blender, combine rice, sesame seeds and the water they were soaked in; blend. Add more water, if needed, to achieve the consistency of smooth cake batter without grains. It may take up to 15 minutes to blend completely.

In a large pot or wok, combine the 8 cups water and brown sugar; bring it to a boil and cook until sugar is dissolved. Lower heat to medium and slowly add the rice/sesame mixture, stirring continuously for 15 to 20 minutes or until mixture thickens.

Serve hot, at room temperature, or cold.

Portuguese Legacy

The delicious small custards served at dim sum restaurants are thought of as Chinese staples, but the custard tradition really hails from Portugal. The art of custard desserts was perfected in Macao, a Portuguese colony, and became so popular that every Chinese dim sum house had to serve them. One theory is that Roman Catholic nuns in Macao used egg whites to starch their habits, leaving many yolks available for other uses, such as custard making. Many Chinese are lactose-intolerant, but cooking the milk, as with a custard, helps ease digestion.

Variation: Substitute shelled peanuts or walnuts for the sesame seeds for a different taste.

Glossary

Abalone, *see* **bao yu**

Abalone sauce, *see* **bao yu jeong**

Aburage, *see* **fried tofu**

Agar agar, *see* **dung yong tsoi**

Arrowroot, *see* **jook woo**

Ba gok
A star-shaped dried spice with a licorice taste used as a flavoring.

Bamboo shoots, *see* **jook sun**

Bao yu
Abalone is an expensive mollusk revered by the Chinese. Available fresh, canned and dried.

Bao yu jeong
A sauce made from abalone extract used for cooking, but more delicate than oyster sauce.

Bean curd skins, *see* **foo jook**

Bean sprouts, *see* **nga choy** *or* **wong dau nga**

Bird's nest, *see* **yin wa**

Bitter melon, *see* **foo gwa**

Black beans, *see* **dau see**

Black mushrooms, *see* **doong gu**

Black vinegar
The strong vinegar used to pickle pig's feet. Its taste is similar to balsamic vinegar.

Bok choy
Called Chinese white cabbage. White stems with green leaves sold in full size, about 7 to 10 inches tall, or as younger "baby bok choy" or Shanghai cabbage about 3 inches tall.

Bok go
Gingko nuts are also called white nuts. Sold canned or fresh with a shell that must be peeled.

Brown bean sauce, *see* **min see jeong**

Bu look
Pomelo is the largest of the citrus fruits, also called jabong in Japanese.

Caul fat, *see* **mong yau**

Cha gwa
Preserved sweet young cucumber used in steamed pork hash or jook.

Chai Pow Yu
A brand of canned gluten, also called min gun. A vegetarian staple.

Char siu
Chinese-style marinated and barbecued red pork.

Chawan mushi
A Japanese savory steamed custard.

Chestnuts, *see* **loo see**

Chicken seasoning powder
A common seasoning used by cooks in modern day China. The first two ingredients are salt and MSG. Also contains dried chicken meat and fat, and many other additives.

Chin yee / ngee
Also called cloud ears or wood ears, or in Hawai'i, pepeiau. A black-gray fungus sold fresh or dried. Bland, but takes on flavors of the sauce and is savored for its crunch.

Chinese bacon, *see* **yin yuk**

Chinese broccoli, *see* **gai lan**

Chinese cabbage, *see* **bok choy** *or* **won bok**

Chinese celery
Looks like a very skinny version of American celery. The taste is the same.

Chinese chives, *see* **gau choy**

Chinese hot mustard, *see* **gai lot**

Chinese okra, *see* **see gwa**

Chinese olive, *see* **lam see**

Chinese parsley, *see* **yin choy**

Chinese raw fish cake
The mixture of minced fish, water and salt that is used in many ways in Chinese cuisine. A clever way of utilizing bony fish.

Chinese red vinegar
Slightly milder than American vinegars; substitute red or white wine vinegar. A condiment enjoyed by Chinese, especially eaten with fried noodles.

Chinese slab sugar, *see* **wong tong**

Chinese taro, *see* **woo tau**

Chinese wine, *see* **shaoxing**

Chung choy
Salted dried turnip, rutabaga, or kohlrabi used as a flavoring ingredient, but usually removed before serving.

Cloud ears, *see* **chin yee**

Congee, *see* **jook**

Cornstarch
Also called corn flour. A thickening agent. Powdered arrowroot, tapioca starch, or flour are also used instead of cornstarch.

Dau foo
A bland protein staple made from soybeans, available fresh, fried, pressed, and in soft or hard textures. Also sold dried in sheets (dau foo pei) or fried.

Dau gok
Long beans or yard-long beans. A round green bean that grows very long and is crispy if not overcooked.

Dau see
Salted, fermented black beans are used to flavor many Southern Chinese dishes, especially in Hakka cuisines.

Doong gu
Also called Chinese mushrooms or shiitake. Sold fresh or dried. Stems are inedible.

Doong gwa
The largest of the Chinese melons, it has dark green skin and white inner meat prized for its sweetness in soups.

Dried cuttlefish, *see* **yau yu**

Dried octopus, *see* **muk yee**

Dried oysters, *see* **hau see**

Dried scallops, *see* **gong yu chu**

Dried shrimp, *see* **ha mai**

Dried tofu, *see* **foo jook**

Dung yong tsoi
Agar agar is a transparent, dried stick made from seaweed and used as a substitute for gelatin.

E foo mein / yee foo mein
Fried, then dried, wheat noodles.

Emein, *see* **e foo mein**

Fa jiu
Formerly Szechuan peppercorns. A dried vegetable, not actually a pepper, that gives a mouth-numbing quality to dishes.

Fan jiu
The coveted crusty rice on the bottom of the rice pot.

Fat choy
The hair-like dried vegetable used in monk's food and other stewed dishes.

Fermented bean paste, *see* **foo yu**

Fermented shrimp sauce, *see* **ham ha**

Fish sauce
A Thai or Vietnamese salty liquid made from fermented fish. Used as a substitute for soy sauce or oyster sauce.

Five-spice powder, *see* **ng heong fun**

Five flowers
A nickname for pork belly.

Foo gwa
Also called balsam pear or bitter gourd, or goya in Okinawan. Resembles a cucumber, but has smooth ridges along its length. Strong bitter taste.

Foo jook
Also tiem jook / foo jook pei. Soybean milk residue made into sheets or dried into sticks. The sheets are simmered with sauce or used as wrappers. The sticks are rehydrated and cooked in stews and soups.

Foo yu / dau foo mui (white)
or nam yue (red)
Also called Chinese cheese. The pungent fermented tofu cubes are sold in bottles and used in stews and stir-fries.

Fried milk
A Chinese dish, said to be invented to make milk digestible to the usually lactose-intolerant Chinese.

Fried tofu
There are two types of fried tofu sold in Hawai'i: blocks of tofu that have a fried exterior and the lighter fried shells that can be stuffed called dau foo pei in Cantonese and aburage in Japanese.

Fuzzy squash, *see* **jit gwa**

Gai lan
Similar to American broccoli, but with longer stems and a more delicate flavor.

Gai lot
A dry spicy mustard that is mixed with water and usually served for dipping with soy sauce. Can substitute English hot mustard.

Gai / kai choy
Also called mustard greens. A bitter green cabbage sold fresh, salted or sweet-pickled (tsin choy).

Gao / Gau, *see* **nien gao**

Garlic chives, *see* **Chinese chives**

Gau choy (green) *or* **gau choy huang (yellow)**
Resembles American chives, but the leaves are flat and not hollow. Also called garlic chives for its garlicky-onion taste. Usually cooked.

Geong
Peeled ginger used as a flavoring.

Ginger, *see* **geong**

Gingko nuts, *see* **bok go**

Go jee
Dried, sweet red berries used in soups and soupy desserts.

Goji berries, *see* **go jee**

Gong yu chu
Expensive delicacy prized for its fishiness. Larger scallops are simmered and served whole. For soup or just flavoring, broken loose segments can be used.

Goong Goong
Grandfather.

Ground or brown bean sauce
Made from fermented soy beans, this is a common cooking sauce used in marinating, steaming, and stir-frying.

Guangdong
Formerly Canton or Kwangtung, a province in southern China bordering the ocean.

Gum choy
Also called golden needles, tiger lily petals, lily buds, or dried tiger lilies. The flower of the day lily, available fresh or dried. Used for its distinctive flavor and tender consistency.

Gum quot
Kumquot is an inch-long, tart orange citrus enjoyed fresh, sugared or preserved in syrup.

Gwa
The generic name for melon. Types of gwa include winter melon, smooth or fuzzy melon, and silk squash.

Gwo pei / pi *or* **chun pei / pi**
The orange-brown dried rind of various fruits used to give a distinctive citrus flavor to soups and meats.

Ha mai
Dried shrimp used to flavor dishes.

Hai sum
Called sea cucumber or beche-de-mer in French. A sea slug sold dried. It has little flavor, but absorbs the taste of the sauce. Considered a delicacy.

Hakka
In Mandarin Chinese, ke jia (without a home). A group of people who migrated from Northern China to southern China in the 12th century, especially to the Guangdong area. The dialect and cooking styles are distinct from the Punti (or local) people.

Ham choy
Salted vegetables.

Ham dan
Duck or chicken eggs salted in brine.

Ham ha
Fermented shrimp paste. A strong, pungent, thick, brownish-pink paste used for flavoring. Similar to Filipino bagoong.

Ham yu
Salted and dried fish, steamed as a main ingredient or mixed with meats as a flavoring. The pungent smell is often offensive to non-Chinese.

Hau jit pei
Dried and shredded jellyfish, sold in packages. Chewy texture enjoyed in salads and appetizers.

Hau / ho see
Fresh oysters or dried uncooked oysters used in stews. Expensive and must be rehydrated.

Hau yau
A thick brown sauce made of oyster essence or extract and soy sauce. One of the most common flavorings; often used as alternative to soy sauce.

Haupia
Hawaiian coconut pudding.

Hoi sin jeong
A sweet, reddish-brown sauce used as a flavoring or a dipping sauce. Made of soybeans, red beans, ginger, garlic, salt, chili, sugar, and spices.

Hoisin sauce, *see* **hoi sin jeong**

Hot bean paste
A thick sauce made from soy beans, but spicier with chili peppers added.

Hot sauce, *see* **lot yau**

Hung jo
Also known as jujubes or red dates. Sold fresh or dried, used in soups and stews to add a mildly sweet flavor. Substitute brown, larger Peking honey dates.

Jah choy
Also called Szechuan vegetable. A rounded knobby root vegetable that is covered with red chili pepper powder.

Jai, *see* **lo han jai**

Jee choy
Dried black sheets of seaweed used in soups.

Jee ma yau
A dark brown oil extracted from toasted sesame seeds used in salads, or as a flavoring in hot dishes just before serving. The flavor dissipates with heat.

Jellyfish, *see* **hau jit pei**

Ji yuk beng
A popular ground pork dish. Now refers to dim sum made with pork hash or to raw ground pork.

Jit gwa *or* **mo gwa**
Smooth-skinned or hairy melon. A vegetable about 8 inches long used as a cooked vegetable or in soups.

Jook
Savory rice gruel or porridge, also called congee.

Jook sun
Young cream-colored shoots of the bamboo plant sold fresh and wrapped in plastic while in season, or salted or pickled in cans. It is also sold dried (called sun ha), and when reconstituted and cooked, has a chewy texture compared to the fresh.

Jook woo
Arrowroot, a white root that resembles bamboo shoots. A favorite vegetable in Zhongshan cooking.

Kim chee
Korean-style vegetables pickled with salt and chili pepper powder.

Kumquat, *see* **gum quot**

Kumu
Hawaiian word for a red goat fish that has very delicate white flesh.

La-ee chi
Also spelled lichee, litchee, or lychee. A red, bumpy-skinned fruit with opaque white, sweet flesh. Available fresh, canned in syrup, and dried.

Lam see *or* **ham lam**
Black or brown cured olives used to flavor vegetables or dim sum.

Li hing mui
A salty sweet dry flavoring powder from China.

Lily flowers, *see* **gum choy**

Lo ba
Chinese turnips are rounder than Japanese turnips. Korean turnips or daikon can be substituted.

Lo han jai
Monk's food, traditionally served during Lunar New Year celebrations.

Long beans *see* **dau gok**

Longan, *see* **loong an**

Loo see
Like the standard American chestnuts and used in stews with chicken, duck, or pork. Not to be confused with water chestnuts.

Loofah squash, *see* **Chinese okra**

Loong an
Meaning dragon's eye. The smooth skin of this fruit is yellow-green or light brown; the inside is opaque, white, and very sweet.

Loquat, *see* **pei pa**

Lot yau
Red condiment made from chili peppers. Many varieties, some with garlic, fermented black beans, sesame oil and chili peppers.

Lotus root, *see* **lyan ngau**

Lotus seeds, *see* **lyan see**

Lup cheong
Chinese sweet pork sausage. Some versions include liver. Reddish-brown with white cubes of fat. Must be cooked.

Lyan ngau
Light brown root of the lotus plant, used in soups and stews; valued for its beautiful design when cut. Available fresh and vacuum-packed.

Lyan see
White, dried seeds of the lotus blossom, available dried or canned.

Lychee, *see* **la-ee chi**

Ma tai
Water chestnuts. Brown-skinned aquatic vegetable with a sweet, crunchy, white interior. Available fresh or canned.

Mai fun
Also called vermicelli. Noodles made from rice that must be soaked, according to the recipe, in hot water before using. They are clear when uncooked and opaque when cooked. There are also Thai rice sticks, which are thicker.

Min gun
Also called vegetable steak or gluten. Sold fresh or in cans with sauce. A staple of the vegetarian kitchen.

Min see jeong
A moist, thick bean paste used as a flavoring.

Mochi rice, *see* **no mai**

Moi
Hawaiian word for threadfish.

Mong yau
Pig's lacy fat, also called caul fat, used to wrap oyster rolls. Available fresh or frozen. Needs to be soaked for long hours to remove the strong smell.

MSG
Monosodium glutamate. Most popular brands are Ve-Tsin in China and Ajinomoto in Japan. Once a popular flavor enhancer, now shunned by many people due to allergies. In older cookbooks, referred to as "gourmet powder." Based on naturally occurring flavor-enhancing chemicals.

Mui
Preserved fruits and vegetables. Any type of "crack seed."

Muk yee
Octopus, used as a strong flavoring ingredient.

Mullet
A fish that is considered good steamed.

Mustard cabbage, *see* **gai choy**

Napa cabbage, *see* **won bok**

Ng heong fun
Five-spice is a popular brown-red flavoring added to many dishes. Usually a mixture of star anise, Chinese cinnamon, fennel, or aniseed, Sichuan peppercorns and cloves, but there are many other combinations.

Nga choy
Mung bean sprouts, usually added to stir-fries at the last minute and appreciated for their crunch.

Nien gao
A steamed sweet rice-flour dessert served during the Lunar New Year.

No mai
Also called sticky rice, sweet rice, glutinous rice or mochi rice. Available as grains or as flour.

Ong choy
Also called kang kong or swamp cabbage. A hollow-stemmed vegetable similar to spinach.

'Ōpakapaka
Hawaiian word for pink snapper.

Orange peel, *see* **tangerine peel**

Oyster sauce, *see* **hau yau**

Pak choy
An alternate way of spelling bok choy.

Peanut oil
Once a favorite for frying, as it can reach a high temperature without burning. Rarely used now because of peanut allergies.

Pei dan
Also called black eggs, 1,000-year-old eggs, 100-year-old eggs. A delicacy usually served with pickled onions or pickled ginger.

Pei pa
Loquat is an oval, orange fruit with a thin skin and sweet orange flesh. Available fresh, canned, and dried.

Pepper salt
A pre-mixed combination of black or white pepper and salt.

Pi or pei
Skin, as in won ton pi or dried tofu sheets.

Plum sauce, *see* **shin mei jeong**

Pomelo, *see* **bu look**

Popo
Grandmother. Maternal grandmother may be called Jia po or Japo.

Pork hash, *see* **ji yuk beng**

Pui tow
Toppings, as for noodles.

Red dates, *see* **hung jo**

Rice sticks, *see* **mai fun**

Sai fun
A cellophane noodle also called glass noodles, or crystal noodles and made from mung bean starch or yam starch. This is the type of noodle for Chicken Long Rice. The noodles have little flavor themselves, but absorb the flavors of soups or stews.

Salted fish, *see* **ham yu**

Sea cucumber, *see* **hai sum**

Seaweed, *see* **jee choy**

See gwa
Also called silk melon, silk squash, loofah squash. The ribbed green skin is peeled to reveal a tender, spongy, white interior.

See yau
Soy sauce is available in dark, light, red, and thick varieties. The fermented sauce made from soy beans is used every day in Chinese cooking. Light soy sauce is used as a flavoring. Dark and thick varieties are used for color.

Sesame oil, *see* **jee ma yau**

Shanghai cabbage, *see* **bok choy**
Alternative name for baby bok choy

Shaoxing wine
The most famous of the yellow rice wines. A cooking wine named after the city in China where it is made. Substitute dry sherry or gin. Other spellings include Hsao Shing, Shaohsing, Shao Hsing.

Shark fin, *see* **yu chi**

Sheng tsai
Mandarin Chinese for lettuce. Soong choy in Cantonese.

Shia dau
Snow peas are also called mange tout (French for "eat all"). A tender, crisp pod that can be eaten whole.

Shin mei jeong
Also called duck or plum sauce. Sweet and sour, purchased in cans or bottles.

Shiso
The leaves of the perilla plant used as a distinct flavor in many Japanese dishes. Also spelled chiso.

Si yong choy
Watercress is sold in small bunches and cooked; may also be eaten raw in salads.

Sichuan peppercorns, *see* **fa jiu**

Snow peas, *see* **shia dau**

Soy beans
A cornerstone of the Chinese diet. An edible legume that is a source of protein. Soybeans are used to make soy sauce, tofu, and many of the sauces used in Chinese food.

Soy sauce, *see* **see yau**

Star anise, *see* **ba gok**

Stem lettuce
A vegetable popular in Beijing for its stem rather than the leaves. Sold in Honolulu's Chinatown markets.

Swamp cabbage, *see* **ong choy**

Sweet rice, *see* **no mai**

Tangerine peel, *see* **gwo pei**

Tatsoi
A dark green Chinese vegetable that is cooked or eaten raw. It is also called rosette bok choy.

Toau
Also called blacktail snapper.

Tofu, *see* **dau foo**

Tsin choy
Sweet pickled mustard cabbage.

Turnip, *see* **lo ba**

Uhu
Hawaiian word for parrotfish.

Umami
The term to describe the pungent, delicious, rich aspect of a dish as in the flavor of mushrooms.

Virginia ham, *see* **Yunnan ham**

Water chestnut, *see* **ma tai**

Watercress, *see* **si yong choy**

White pepper
A version of black pepper with a lighter taste. Common in Chinese cooking.

Winter melon, *see* **doong gwa**

Won bok
Also called Chinese celery cabbage or tientsin bai tsai. Green and yellow with white stalks, this is a staple vegetable.

Wong dau nga
Soy bean sprouts are used in stir-fries.

Wong tong
Light brown or dark brown cane sugar sold in sticks or slabs. Substitute brown sugar.

Tin Tin Chop Suey in Chinatown, Honolulu.

Woo tau
A Chinese land taro that is drier when cooked compared with Hawaiian varieties. White-gray on the inside, it has a mild flavor, but absorbs flavors of the sauce.

Wood ears, *see* **cloud ears**

XO sauce
A seasoned, strong-flavored sauce made from seafood, including scallops and shrimp, that is used in stir-fry dishes.

Yau yu
Dried squid used to flavor soups and ground pork.

Yin choy
Chinese parsley also called fresh coriander or cilantro. The strong-flavored flat-leafed parsley has a distinct taste that people either love or hate.

Yin wa
Bird's nest is a dried delicacy made from the saliva of cliff-dwelling swallows. Very expensive and served only at banquets. Must soak and clean before making into soups or desserts.

Yin yuk
Smoked pork belly used to flavor dishes.

Yu chi
Shark's fin was once an expensive delicacy treasured for its gelatinous texture. Banned for sale in many locales due to concern over cruelty in fishing methods.

Yunnan ham
Famous salty dry ham similar to Virginia, Smithfield, or country hams in the United States. Yunnan is also known as Kunming province in China.

Glossary

Index

About the Author

Lynette Claire Lian Fu Lo Tom (羅蓮富) is the eldest child of Richard Cheong Lo and Lorna Lee Lo. Her grandparents were Tan and Louise Ho Lo and John (Duck) Sau and Florence Wong Lee. Growing up in Makiki and Mānoa with her sisters Joanne and Charlene and her brothers Russell and Barry, she ate Chinese food almost every day and always appreciated its variety. She is an enthusiastic home cook. Lynette is a proud graduate of Mānoa Elementary, Stevenson Intermediate and Punahou School. She earned a journalism degree from University of Colorado at Boulder and an MBA from the University of California at Berkeley. A former reporter, she created a successful public relations and marketing firm, Bright Light Marketing. Now she is focusing on the culinary world with her company Bright Light Cookery and is especially fascinated by foods cooked "back in the day." She enjoys living in Honolulu and always finds excuses to cook. Lynette is married to Neal Kanda and has a daughter Jenny, stepson Sean, and granddaughter Chloe. Contact Lynette at lynette@brightlightcookery.com.

The photographs for this book were taken at Leeward Community College with the enthusiastic assistance of students from an Asian/continental cuisine class at LCC. The students tested the recipes and prepared each dish for its moment in the spotlight. Many thanks to chef-instructor David Millen, whose efficiency and wealth of knowledge kept us on track each day.

Other Titles in the Series

A *Korean Kitchen* explores a popular cuisine that relies on many vegetables, grains, fermented foods, and simple cooking techniques that require little fat. Meats are served as a small part of this vegetable-centric cuisine that focuses on many tasty side dishes on the table. Food writer Joan Namkoong draws on her island heritage to explain the Korean kitchen in Hawai'i, distinctly different from a Korean kitchen in Korea.

180 pp. • 6 x 9 in. • Hardcover

A *Portuguese Kitchen* shares traditional recipes done Hawai'i-style by Wanda A. Adams. Portuguese cooking is at its heart very, very simple. The cuisine relies on the freshest, most carefully selected ingredients. It is comforting, but not edgy, earthy, sumptuous, and tasty. Find recipes for traditional Bacalhau (salt cod), Portuguese soup, Linguica Pica (spicy Portuguese sausage), Arroz Verde (Green Rice), Milho Frito (Fried Cornmeal Porridge), and more.

192 pp. • 6 x 9 in. Hardcover

An *Okinawan Kitchen* features the vibrancy of Okinawan cuisine—with all the heartiness of pork cooked many ways, the brightness of bitter melon and eggplant, and the purity of tofu prepared from scratch. This book is for those with Okinawan roots who seek to finally master classic rafute (braised pork) and goya champuru (bitter melon stir-fry) and for the adventurous cook willing to discover new takes on Okinawan flavors.

164 pp. • 6 x 9 in. Hardcover

To order these titles and more, visit
www.mutualpublishing.com

Notes

_____
_____
_____
_____
_____
_____
_____
_____
_____
_____
_____
_____

Jade vine